Maine
THE WAY LIFE SHOULD BE

A photo portrait of the pine tree state

Collecting lobster traps in Casco Bay.
Theodora Medouris | Portland

© Copyright 2012 New England Business Media, LLC

ISBN 978-0-615-67259-5
Library of Congress Control Number: 2012912552

A publication of:
New England Business Media, LLC
Mainebiz
2 Cotton Street, 3rd Floor, Portland, ME 04101

Group publisher: Joe Zwiebel
Publisher and editor: Leila Musacchio
Publishing consultant: Donna Brassard
Photo editors: Bruce Brown, Greta Rybus
Profile writer: Heather Douglas
Copy editor: Jessica Skwire Routhier
Art director: Jan Holder
Graphic designers: Dave Harford, Matt Selva
Special projects: Shay Bellas, Ken Hanson, Barbara Kenney, Betsy VanderPloeg
Project coordinators: Jenna Grant, Christina Rouse

Distributed by Mainebiz, www.mainebiz.biz
Printed in the U.S.A. by Taylor Specialty Books, Naugatuck, Connecticut

The Profiles in Excellence were written and approved by the individual companies.
The profiles may not reflect the opinions or editorial styles of Mainebiz or
New England Business Media.

....

The popular hiking destination Tumbledown Mountain.

Chris Lawrence | Scarborough

Contents

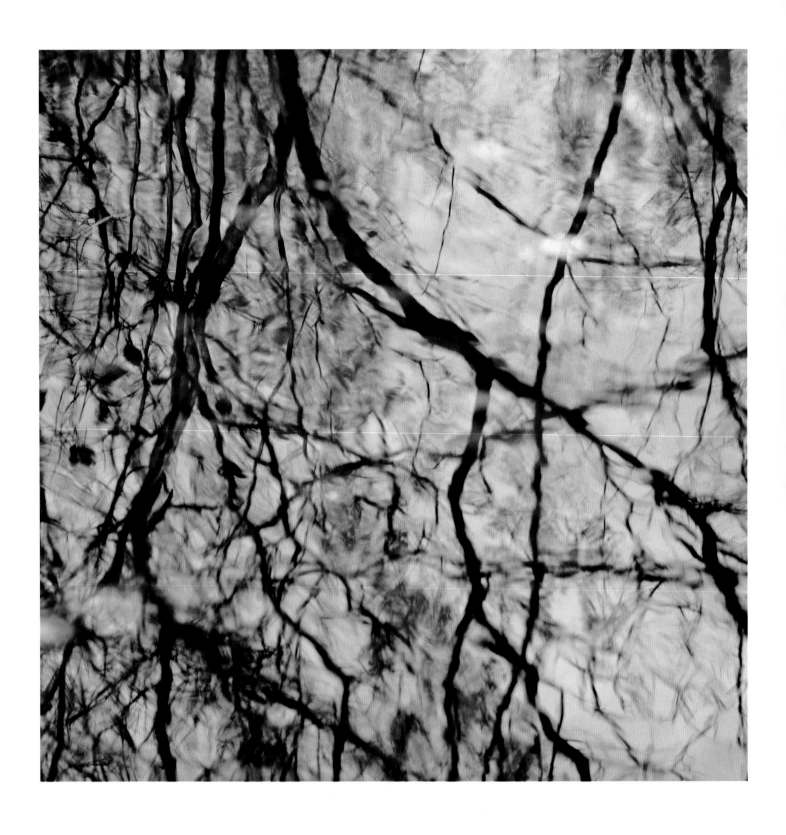

Reflections of a tree at Wild Gardens of Acadia, Acadia National Park.

Jim Nickelson | Camden

Welcome to Maine

People come from all over the world to see what all the fuss is about; to learn why Maine is "the way life should be." And while we lovingly throw open our doors, walking trails, and coastlines to our guests, there's more to Maine than a quick visit. You could spend a lifetime here: raising your kids, growing your business, and living the way you've always dreamed. In fact, some have called Maine's quality of life the "best in the nation.[1]"

The romance of living here is sometimes hard to imagine, for those who haven't yet. Laughing as you watch your children chase after fireflies aglow in your backyard, biking to the closest beach[2], armed with sandwiches, sunscreen, and a Frisbee. Having enough room to grow a garden or enjoying dinner with friends at a restaurant that features fresh, locally and sustainably grown foods. Making last-minute plans with friends to go hiking, kayaking, or sailing because it's so easy to access nature from wherever you are in Maine. Just open your door.

It's true that we revel in our small-town customs, like Yarmouth's Clam Festival or Damariscotta's Pumpkin Festival (complete with annual Pumpkin Regatta). We're completely shameless about our Main Street parades and farmers' markets, as well as our agricultural fairs (like Common Ground Country Fair and Fryeburg Fair). The Caribou Winter Carnival makes light of the chill with a month full of winter fun.

While we love our heritage, and some of us can trace family roots further back than our statehood in 1820, many of us came here looking for something better. A way of life. Some Mainers are well-known artists, writers, musicians, and innovative entrepreneurs (Stephen King, Patrick Dempsey, Judd Nelson, E.B. White, Andrew Wyeth), but most of us are everyday, hard-working people.

We like our small-town sports development teams and expect to see people we know when we catch a ballgame on a Tuesday evening after work. We see our own players join the ranks of the Celtics and Red Sox, and we're proud that we saw them here first.

Here in Maine, we have seasons. All four of them. And each with its own promise of adventure. Those seasons mark the beauty of passing time and the charm of change; from the blooming of the Azalea Gardens in Northeast Harbor to the return of the ducks to Deering Oaks Park pond. When the days get shorter and snow begins to fly, we give ourselves permission to live differently: telecommuting to the office or taking the day to go sledding with our kids.

While we may enjoy the people and landscape around us as we're doing it, Mainers are full of entrepreneurial spirit. In fact, 14% of Mainers over 18 own a business[3]. We're famous for the things we make, because craftsmanship is something we take seriously. You can see it in our boat building, beer crafting, and everyone's favorite L.L.Bean boots. Our own Portland ranks fifth in the nation for being the best place to launch a small business[4]. We have competitive labor costs[5], state-funded work force training, and tons of incentives[6]. We're in the right spot, too, with three commercial deepwater ports, an intermodal rail facility with a free trade zone, multiple modern airports, and affordable real estate with same-day access to Boston, New York and Montreal.

In fact, we export our share of goods to neighbors as close as Canada and as far as New Zealand. Our top exports by industry include computers and electronic products, paper, and transportation equipment[7]. Our work force is educated, and we're home to more than 35 colleges and universities, both public and private. We have state-of-the-art health care facilities, among them the Harold Alfond Cancer Center, Maine Center for Cancer Medicine, Maine Heart Center, and Barbara Bush Children's Hospital.

Maine embraces research and development. For example, Maine Technology Institute offers commercialization grants and early stage financing for R&D projects. State university innovation centers foster advancements in life sciences, renewable energy, and advanced materials. We're home to world-class research facilities, including The Jackson Laboratory, The Gulf of Maine Research Institute, Mount Desert Island Biological Laboratory, Bigelow Laboratory, and University of Maine's AEWC Advanced Structures and Composites Center.

Whether it's our coveted quality of life, rich culture, vibrant commerce, or bright future, you'll see in these pages just a slice of what we have to offer. So come see for yourself. Whether for a visit or a lifetime, the reasons to join us may be endless.

Leila Musacchio, publisher and editor

1 fDi Editor, "Best quality of life," fDi Intelligence, The Financial Times LTD, 6 Jul. 2005, http://www.fdiintelligence.com/Archive/Best-quality-of-life (accessed June 2012).

2 Maine's landscape includes 5,500 miles of coastline, 6,000 lakes and world-class sustainable forests, according to Maine's Department of Economic and Community Development.

Maine.gov, "Maine Department of Economic and Community Development," Maine.gov, http://www.maine.gov/decd/ (accessed June 2012).

3 United State Census Bureau, "State Characteristics: Vintage 2011," U.S. Department of Commerce, http://www.census.gov/popest/data/state/asrh/2011/index.html (accessed 12 Jun. 2012).

Small Business Administration: Office of Advocacy, "Small Business Profile: Maine," U.S. Small Business Administration, Office of Advocacy, http://www.sba.gov/sites/default/files/me11_0.pdf (accessed 12 Jun. 2012).

United States Census Bureau, "Estimates of the Resident Population by Selected Age Groups for the United States, States, and Puerto Rico," U.S. Department of Commerce http://www.census.gov/popest/data/state/asrh/2011/tables/SC-EST2011-01.xls (accessed 12 Jun. 2012).

4 Upstart Business Journal, "Small Business Vitality 2010," Upstart Business Journal, http://upstart.bizjournals.com/multimedia/interactives/2010/01/small-business-vitality-2010.html (accessed July 2012).

5 Competitive labor costs at 6% less than the national per capita rate. Maine.gov, "Maine Department of Economic and Community Development," Maine.gov, http://www.maine.gov/decd/ (accessed June 2012).

6 See http://www.maine.gov/decd for incentives. Award-winning tax incentive Pine Tree Development Zone program. Nationally recognized Community Development Block Grant program provides funds to projects including infrastructure development. Progressive tax reimbursement policies. Maine.gov, "Maine Department of Economic and Community Development," Maine.gov, http://www.maine.gov/decd/ (accessed June 2012).

7 Mainebiz Fact Book, 2 Jul. 2012.

Ice fishing shack.
Scott Peterman | Hollis

Man digging for clams in an East Blue Hill cove.

Françoise Gervais | Blue Hill

Sarah and Kobi feed birds at Schoodic Point in Acadia National Park.

Gifford Ewing | Sorrento

Browsing the children's section at Second Read Books & Coffee in Rockland.
David McLain | Aurora Photos | North Yarmouth

Nigel Chase and his high school steel drum band, Planet Pan, performing at a steel drum music festival.
Alexandria Brahler | Portland

Emily Rothschild and Jon Retseck at their home in Small Point. From the series "Are you really my friend? The Facebook portrait project."
Tanja Hollander | Auburn

Homes on South Portland's Cedar Street during a snowstorm.
Mark Marchesi | South Portland

Tristan reads on his way to school from Vinalhaven.
Bridget Besaw | Aurora Photos | Portland

A high school student gets in a little homework before dress rehearsal.
Bridget Besaw | Aurora Photos | Portland

A volunteer helps dig out parked cars during a big snowstorm in Portland's Bayside neighborhood.
Alexander Kreher | Portland

Children playing backyard hockey in Camden behind a home designed by Eric Allyn, architectural designer, and Phi Home Design.

Brian Vanden Brink | Rockport

Mel Smith and Doug Drew performing at the Every Friday Coffee House and Open Mic, Riverside Park in Presque Isle.
William Lloyd Duncan | Stockholm

The fishing village of Stonington on Deer Isle.
Cynthia Farr-Weinfeld | Portland

Children wait in anticipation at the annual Youth Concert presented by the Portland Symphony Orchestra at Portland's Merrill Auditorium.
Diane Hudson | Portland

Earth at Hidden Pond, a "Farm to Fork" restaurant.
Trent Bell | Portland

Floyd and Bethany at Green Memorial African Methodist Episcopal Zion Church in Portland.

Sean Harris | Portland

Portland's historic U.S. Custom House was built in 1867 to support Maine's growing customs business.

Jan Pieter van Voorst van Beest | Pownal

Blueberry fields at the base of Vienna Mountain.

John Orcutt | Aurora Photos | Kingfield

Sandy Pearson and Cynthia Orcutt pick wild cranberries at the boggy edge of Richarson Lake.

John Orcutt | Aurora Photos | Kingfield

Boys playing football in Augusta.
Matt Cosby | Rockport

At Slates in Hallowell.

Jan Pieter van Voorst van Beest | Pownal

A boy doing a headstand in Northport.
Brendan Bullock | Montville

A boy celebrating Independence Day at Sebago Lake.

Laura 'Winky' Lewis | Portland

At Portland's monthly, year-round First Friday Art Walk.
Corey Templeton | Portland

A child chases kite tails at the Bug Lite Kite Festival in South Portland.

Diane Hudson | Portland

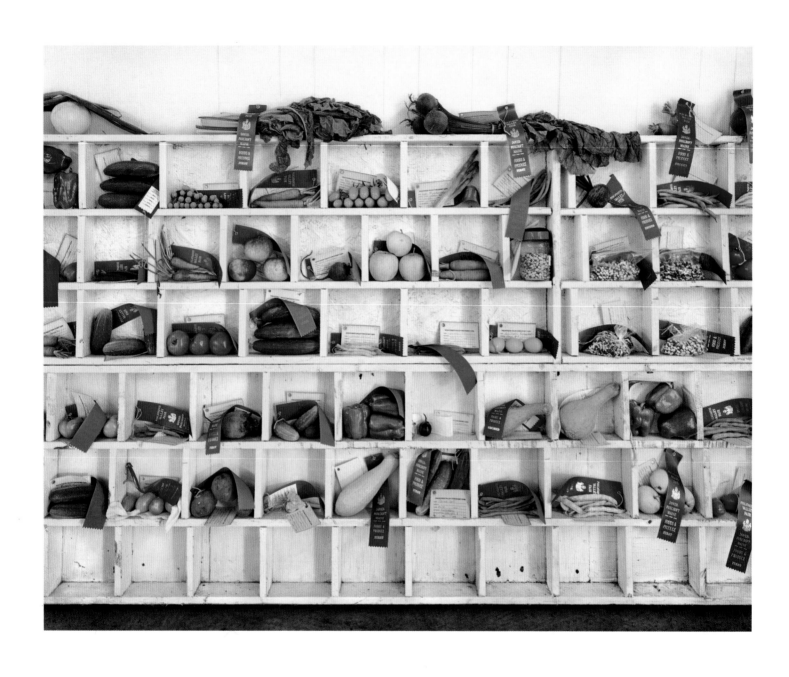

Prize-winning vegetables at the Piscataquis Valley Fair, Dover-Foxcroft.

Thomas Birtwistle | Harmony

Harvesting organic produce at the Six Rivers Farm near Bowdoinham.

Bridget Besaw | Aurora Photos | Portland

Hot dog vendor at Monument Square, Portland.
Lauren Kennedy | Portland

Two young girls in Portland's Old Port.
Laura "Winky" Lewis | Aurora Photos | Portland

People dancing in Portland's Old Port.

Chris Lawrence | Scarborough

Three generations share a family meal together in North Yarmouth.
David McLain | Aurora Photos | North Yarmouth

Bowdoin College sophomore, Brooks Crowe, studies in secluded Hubbard Hall on the Brunswick campus.

Carl D. Walsh | Aurora Photos | Portland

Brian Ború is one of Portland's most popular pubs.

Chris Lawrence | Scarborough

Passengers disembark the ferry at Casco Bay Ferry Terminal in Portland.

José Azel | Aurora Photos | Lovell

Groups of pirates from Eastport invade Lubec the week before the Eastport Pirate Festival.
Don Dunbar | Perry

A biathlete at Nordic Heritage Center in Fort Fairfield.

Stephen Leighton | Fort Fairfield

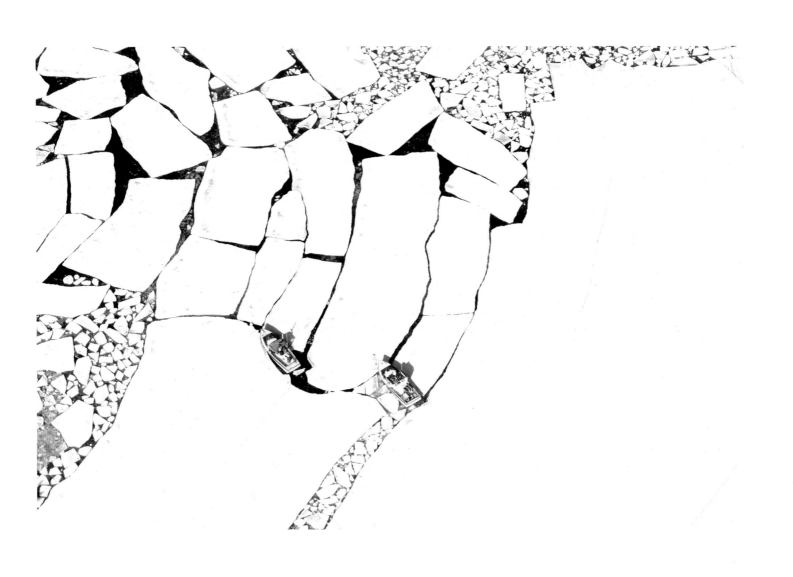

Lobster boats stuck in ice off Deer Isle.
Ben Magro | Appleton

Farm buildings in Presque Isle.
Paul Cyr | Presque Isle

During the holiday season, abstract light sculptures designed by Pandora LaCasse decorate downtown Portland.
Peter Bissell | Portland

Swimming in a heated outdoor pool at the Grand Summit Resort Hotel at Sunday River ski resort in Newry.
David McLain | Aurora Photos | North Yarmouth

Shelly Thorp and Anita Day during the annual New Year's Eve Polar Bear Plunge, an event to raise funds to combat global warming, East End Beach, Portland.

Tim Greenway | Portland

A sled dog team racing down Main Street at Fort Kent.

Paul Cyr | Presque Isle

Terri alpine skis with support from volunteer instructor Dennis Doyon at Sunday River ski resort. Maine Adaptive Sports & Recreation provides adaptive ski lessons to children and adults with physical disabilities, free of charge.

Eric Topper | Maine Adaptive Sports & Recreation | Newry

Snowmobiles and groomers on Coburn Mountain.
The Forks Area Chamber of Commerce | West Forks

Rafting down the Kennebec River.
The Forks Area Chamber of Commerce | West Forks

Hikers ascend the Cathedral Trail toward Baxter Peak on Mount Katahdin.
Peter Bissel | Portland

A camper starts a fire before an incoming storm at the Junior Maine Guide testing site in Oquossoc.
Birch Rock Camp | Waterford

Tourists at Pemaquid Point.
Brendan Bullock | Montville

Mother and daughter acrobats, the Flying Wallendas, perform at the Union Fair.
Brendan Bullock | Montville

The starting line for the men's professional bike race at the annual Yarmouth Clam Festival.

Yarmouth Clam Festival | Yarmouth

An ornithology class observes the warbler's spring migration at College of the Atlantic.

College of the Atlantic | Bar Harbor

Paddlers prepare for moonlight canoeing through Scarborough Marsh.
Tim Greenway | Portland

Mark Synnott climbs *Sedated (5.11c)* above the Atlantic in Acadia National Park.

David McLain | Aurora Photos | North Yarmouth

Captain Daniel Bennet and crew during the Eggemoggin Reach Regatta.
Dee Peppe | Rockland

Beachgoers and tourists at Old Orchard Beach.

Liv Kristin Robinson | Belfast

Kids cooling off in Baxter State Park's Daicey Pond.

Carol Liscovitz | Brunswick

The Moore Camps, nestled between Midday and Sunset Ponds, were built as summer homes in the early 1900s.
Roger Merchant | Glenburn

Dancers from Vanga Inanga, a Rwandan dance troupe, perform outside the Museum of African Culture at the annual Kwenu Celebration in Portland.
Diane Hudson | Portland

The 1807 Portland Observatory, now a museum, is the last remaining maritime signal station in the United States.

Bill Hall | Greater Portland Landmarks, Inc. | Portland

A young child with a lobster at the Yarmouth Clam Festival.

Yarmouth Clam Festival | Yarmouth

A hot air balloon launch during the Great Falls Balloon Festival in Auburn.
Celeste Cota | Brewer

Kate Shaffer, co-owner of Black Dinah Chocolatiers, decorates wild raspberry truffles in the company's kitchen on Isle au Haut.
Stacey Cramp | Portland

The chapel at Sabbathday Lake Shaker Village, New Gloucester.
Craig M. Becker | Windham

Jam band, moe., performs at the Maine State Pier in Portland.

Tim Greenway | Portland

USS Jason Dunham, constructed at Bath Iron Works, in drydock ready for float-off.
General Dynamics Bath Iron Works | Bath

The Port Authorities Roller Derby Team, based in Portland, is ranked in the top ten in the East.
Brian Fitzgerald | Aurora Photos | Portland

Nancy Stark Smith, one of the originators of contact improv, teaches a class at the Bates Dance Festival.
Arthur Fink | Portland

Artist Richard Lee standing in his studio in the Ames Mill, Richmond.
Christine Macchi | Dresden

Peter Frampton performs "Something's Happening" to a sold-out crowd at the State Theatre in Portland.
Tim Greenway | Portland

A visitor views paintings at the Portland Museum of Art.
Tim Greenway | Portland

The ceviche roll at Portland's Miyake Restaurant.
Stacey Cramp | Portland

Conductor Lucas Richman acknowledges Trond Saeverud before a performance at the Bangor Symphony Orchestra.
Bangor Symphony Orchestra | Bangor

Piano in Portland's Merrill Auditorium, with architectutural design by Winton Scott.

Brian Vanden Brink | Rockport

The South Solon Meeting House is covered in frescoes that were painted in the 1950s by painters at the Skowhegan School of Painting and Sculpture.
Thomas Birtwistle | Harmony

The Olson House, located in Cushing and famously painted by Andrew Wyeth, is a popular summer tourist destination operated by the Farnsworth Museum in Rockland.
Brian Vanden Brink | Rockport

The award-winning Haystack Mountain School of Crafts' campus buildings, designed by Edward Larrabee Barnes.
Haystack Mountain School of Crafts | Deer Isle

Dancers at the Maine State Ballet perform "Serenade," choreography by George Balanchine. © The George Balanchine Trust.

Maine State Ballet | Falmouth

Rockland's Main Street with the Farnsworth Art Museum on the left. The "Eat" sign on top of the Farnsworth was created by Robert Indiana.
Heath Paley | Arundel

Student Max Hurwitz in his studio space at the Maine College of Art, located in Portland's arts district.

Maine College of Art | Portland

The foyer at Portland's Victoria Mansion, also known as the Morse-Libby House, built in 1858.
Brian Vanden Brink | Rockport

Lawrence Hill of the Portland Red Claws, right, tips the ball away from Luke Zeller of the Austin Toros in a basketball game at the Portland Expo.
Tim Greenway | Portland

Migrant workers harvest broccoli in Presque Isle.

Paul Cyr | Presque Isle

Potato planting in Mars Hill.
Paul Cyr | Presque Isle

Jamaican apple pickers in Auburn.
Brendan Bullock | Montville

Silo and fences at Pineland Farms, New Gloucester.

Jo Chaney | Scarborough

Portland community members network during TEDxDirigo, an indepedently organized TED event designed to spread ideas, Abromson Community Education Center at the University of Southern Maine, Portland.

Michael Eric Berube | TEDxDirigo

The interior of the Maine State House, Augusta.

Cynthia Farr-Weinfeld | Portland

A production employee at Sebasticook Farms Lumber Mill, St. Albans.

Tim Greenway | Portland

Hilary Ritt turns a bowl on a lathe at the Center for Furniture Craftsmanship, Rockport.
Center for Furniture Craftsmanship | Rockport

Erika Soule, owner of Rock Paper Scissors in downtown Wiscasset.

Greta Rybus | Portland

Chef Krista Kern Desjarlais, owner of Bresca in Portland.
Karl Schatz | Portland

An Allagash Brewing Company employee rinses an area in the brewery, Portland.
Tim Greenway | Portland

Potato harvest in Caribou.

Carl D. Walsh | Aurora Photos | Portland

The gown room at National Semiconductor in South Portland.
Jeffrey Stevensen | Aurora Photos | Portland

Both wild and farmed blueberries are grown in Maine.

Thomas Birtwistle | Portland

Eliot Coleman and Barbara Damrosch collect eggs in a rolling greenhouse that houses hens during the winter, fertilizing fields.
Stacey Cramp | Portland

Allen West of Tenants Harbor, deckhand, steam cleans the hull of the *Ella Christine* at the pier in Port Clyde.
Jeffrey Stevensen | Portland

Daadir Aweis, a medical student, works at the Al-Amin Halaal Market in Portland. Aweis moved to Maine from Somalia in 2004.
Greta Rybus | Portland

Elizabeth Neptune, a member of Passamaquoddy Tribal Council, speaks about health, wellness and tribal culture at TEDxDirigo, Hannaford Hall at the University of Southern Maine, Portland.
Michael Eric Berube | TEDxDirigo

Luke Livingston is the CEO of Baxter Brewing Co. in Lewiston.
Peter Bissell | Portland

Men loading bait on a lobster boat in South Thomaston.
Peter Ralston | Rockport

Kurt Durand heaves fish into a bucket as he unloads the day's catch.
Tim Greenway | Portland

Fishermen working at the Municipal Fish Pier, Rockland.
Ni Rong | Rockport

Rajesh Mandekar is the chef at Tulsi, an inventive Indian restaurant in Kittery.
Stacey Cramp | Portland

Antonio Zamora, José Salud Arias Zamora and Raoul Arias take a break from picking blueberries.

Kris Larson | East Machias

The Amtrak Downeaster runs from Portland to Boston five times daily.

Tim Greenway | Portland

Sheep towed in a dory through Penobscot Bay.
Peter Ralston | Rockport

Beach at Reid State Park, Georgetown.

Whitney Fox | Peaks Island

Profiles in Excellence

The profiles to follow represent a dynamic and vital group in Maine's economy. They bring prosperity as well as civic, social and human connections to our state.

Each organization has a story to tell, and it is here that those stories are shared; in their own words. Arranged by the date of founding, these profiles chronicle the strong commitment business and industry have exhibited – and continue to contribute – toward the well-being and quality of life here in Maine.

Companies listed by year founded

The University of Maine

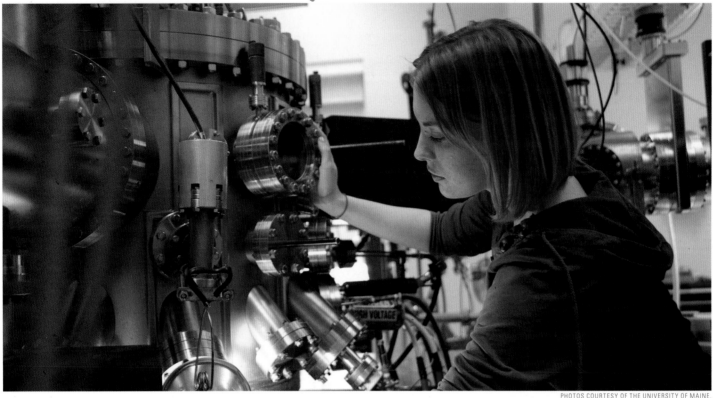

The University of Maine is the state's only university ranked in Tier 1 of America's Top National Universities.

University of Maine has a statewide mission of teaching, research and public service, and it is dedicated to addressing the educational, economic, cultural and social needs of the state.

Founded in Orono in 1865, the University of Maine is among the most comprehensive higher education institutions in the Northeast, attracting students from across the U.S. and more than 80 countries. It currently enrolls 11,200 undergraduate and graduate students, with more than 2,000 students graduating from the university annually.

UMaine is the state's largest public research institution with a mission of teaching, research and service. Here, students find the extensive academic opportunities expected from a major university with the close-knit feel of a small college. As Maine's flagship university, UMaine offers more than 90 undergraduate majors and academic programs, 75 master's programs and 30 doctoral programs. Top students are invited to join UMaine's Honors College, one of the country's oldest honors programs.

The University of Maine is one of *The Princeton Review*'s best 376 colleges, a *Forbes* Top College and Maine's only university that is ranked in Tier 1 of America's Top National Universities by *U.S. News and World Report*. The Carnegie Foundation for the Advancement of Teaching ranks UMaine in the top 8 percent of colleges and universities classified as a "Research University-High Research Activity" institution.

As Maine's land-grant and sea-grant institution, the University of Maine addresses the educational, economic, cultural and social needs of the state. While the University of Maine campus is in Orono, its impact can be felt in every corner of Maine and throughout the world.

The university's commitment to lifelong learning includes its statewide outreach through Cooperative Extension, which operates 16 county Cooperative Extension offices and two outreach centers: the Darling Marine Center in Walpole and the Hutchinson Center in Belfast.

UMaine is one of the National Science Foundation's top 100 research universities, and our facilities and faculty have an international reputation for excellence. Among the highlights are the Climate Change Institute, which has been featured on "60 Minutes," the Laboratory for Surface Science and Technology, a hub for cutting-edge sensor and nanotechnology research, the Advanced Structures & Composites Center, leading the nation in deepwater offshore wind energy development, and the Forest Bioproducts Research Institute, exploring sustainable biofuel alternatives.

UMaine conducts research and development initiatives in all seven of the state's designated technology sectors. In fact, UMaine is the only research institution in Maine to include large-scale, pilot-plant capabilities to demonstrate and commercialize real-scale R&D. Related research areas and facilities include pulp and paper and forest bioproducts, wood composites and structural composites, food, aquaculture, nanotechnology (clean room), advanced manufacturing, supercluster supercomputing, and agriculture. Maine companies partner with UMaine and regularly use these facilities for their business development needs.

UMaine's inventory of high-tech specialized equipment is shared with research institutions throughout Maine. In the 2011 fiscal year, UMaine's Target Technology Incubator provided space to 12 tenant companies, supported nine affiliate companies and provided referrals or counseling to more than 200 companies and entrepreneurs. UMaine-affiliated aquaculture incubators in Franklin and Walpole supported four companies moving toward full-scale commercialization. In addition, four new tech-based start-up companies formed to commercialize UMaine patent-pending technology.

The Foster Center for Student Innovation is nurturing Maine's next generation of high-tech entrepreneurs and innovators. The center is currently partnering with Eureka! Ranch, the National Institute of Standards and Technology, and the Maine Manufacturing Extension Partnership to develop a National Innovation Marketplace.

At the University of Maine, undergraduate research is a priority and a point of pride. Students publish, travel and work alongside UMaine's world-class scholars and scientists. The Center for Undergraduate Research was established in 2008 to connect students with faculty projects that suit their interests. The Division of Lifelong Learning offers online classes and distance-learning opportunities for students who need a flexible class schedule.

In addition to research, UMaine students have extraordinary opportunities to gain real-world, hands-on experience in and out of the classroom. SPIFFY, a student investment club, manages a $1.6 million real-money portfolio. Wildlife ecology majors learn about bear behavior by going out and tagging cubs. Engineering majors take advantage of co-ops and internships that often lead to employment after graduation. Education majors take advantage of urban, rural and international student-teaching opportunities.

UMaine is committed to its public service programs and departments, involvement in public schools, and continuing education opportunities. Here, students have opportunities to work alongside some of the most renowned scholars and scientists in the world — whether they're talking civil engineering with their professors over dinner at Pat's Pizza or traversing an Antarctic ice sheet with researchers from UMaine's Climate Change Institute.

Remarkable opportunities for learning and discovery are provided in UMaine's state-of-the-art research and classroom facilities. In addition, the University of Maine is home to the region's cultural hub, the Collins Center for the Arts, as well as several museums and galleries. The School of Performing Arts and Department of Art are among the strongest forces in the academic arts in the state. The University of Maine Museum of Art has the largest fine arts collection owned entirely by the people of Maine. The Hudson Museum has one of the finest collections of pre-Columbian artifacts in North America. The Page Farm and Home Museum celebrates Maine's history of farms and farming communities.

UMaine also is home to Fogler Library, the state's largest library, which houses approximately 1 million volumes, subscribes to over 4,000 periodicals and serial titles, and serves as a depository for over 2.2 million government documents.

For extracurriculars, students can get involved in more than 200 clubs and organizations — academic and social — one of 17 fraternities or seven sororities, Student Government, community service-oriented groups, intramural sports and much more. UMaine is the state's only Division I school, and athletic events — especially hockey — are a big part of student life here. In fact, the *Wall Street Journal* says Alfond Arena has the best atmosphere in college hockey, and Orono is ranked 29 in *The Bleacher Report*'s Top 50 Hockey Cities in North America.

UMaine is one of the top 100 public universities nationwide for research, with recent annual research expenditures totalling more than $100 million.

The University of Maine's historic buildings include Fogler Library on the Mall, Maine's largest library.

Wyman's of Maine

August harvest on the Barrens.

"We understood the concept of 'continuous improvement,' or 'Kaizen' in Japanese, due to our success in that market. Sustainability was nothing more than applying continuous improvement to how we manage our natural and human resources."

Jasper Wyman opened a seafood canning plant in Milbridge, Maine in 1874. Not long thereafter he also began canning the wild blueberries found along the coast and the barrens of Downeast Maine. Now, nearly 140 years later, Wyman's is the premier marketer of Maine's wild blueberry crop. Still proudly owned by the Wyman family, the company farms 10,000 acres of wild blueberry fields and processes the berries at two processing facilities in Maine and Prince Edward Island, Canada.

Wild blueberries are "wild" because they've never been planted. They are from a root system that is indigenous to the thin sandy soil of glacial Maine and date back many hundreds of years. Wild blueberries are known as "lowbush" blueberries due to their low-to-ground stature. They are one of North America's three native fruits (along with cranberries and concord grapes).

Native Americans noticed that wild blueberries grew better after forest fires and thus adopted the practice of setting fires to the land to clear competing vegetation. While this practice has been largely replaced by mowing the land after harvest, it demonstrates the primary role of the grower to be one of managing, rather than planting, the crop. Each wild blueberry field possesses many different clones which provide the crop with their unique sweet/tart flavor. Some are sweeter than others, some are more tart. Some are lighter in color and some are very dark. But it always averages out blue and delicious.

Wild blueberries only crop every two years. Thus in any given year, half of Wyman's land is bearing fruit and the other half is sprouting and developing buds for the following year. Wild blueberries adapted to the long winters/short summers of Maine, and the best crop is one where the buds have a nice snow blanket protecting them from the winter winds. This is followed by a spring warm enough to open the buds into small white flowers.

Wyman's then places 2-3 bee hives per acre into the fields (taking care to protect those hives from the bears) and hopefully in the warm sunshine of May the bees will go about their busy work and pollinate the crop. Little green berries form almost as soon as the bees leave, and since a ripe blueberry will be about 88% water and 12% solids (mostly sugar and fiber) Wyman's fields need about one inch of water per week during the June-August growing and harvesting period. What Mother Nature doesn't provide, Wyman's can partially replace via irrigation systems in that short growing season.

The harvest generally runs the month of August and is finished by Labor Day. In addition to Wyman's 140 full-time Maine employees, another 500+ seasonal workers are hired. Wild blueberries were harvested by hand until the late 1990s, but now most are harvested by machines. Because of the low-to-ground plants and the harvest practices, very little of the wild blueberry crop sells as fresh produce. Virtually the entire crop is processed — cleaned, washed and frozen. The fac-

"I see sustainability as a way forward that respects all of our stakeholders and in time will pay off with like-minded customers. As our tag line says, we are recommended by future generations," says President & CEO Ed Flanagan.

Top: Harvesting machines on the Barrens.

Bottom: Wyman's of Maine retail products.

tories continuously process the crop, which means between 1-1.5 million pounds. of fruit each day run through Wyman's factories.

For many years wild blueberries were primarily used for "muffins-pies-pancakes" in the U.S. and for jams and yogurts in Europe and Japan. But during the 1990s the USDA's Aging & Nutrition Center at Tufts University developed a methodology for quantifying the antioxidant values in fruits and vegetables, and blueberries ranked number one. Lab studies verified the benefits of antioxidants, especially the antioxidant properties of blueberries found mostly in the blue color. Research at many universities developed positive findings for blueberries and its antioxidant, anti-cancer, anti-inflammatory and anti-aging properties. The wild blueberry has evolved characteristics that it needed to survive growing low to the ground in a harsh climate. And it is those characteristics that are behind the healthy reputation of wild blueberries. As a result, per capita blueberry consumption over the last decade has more than doubled.

Wyman's is the number-one brand of frozen blueberry in the U.S., selling at traditional groceries, natural food stores and warehouse clubs. Wyman's also sells wild blueberry juice, canned fruit and other frozen berries to the retail trade. Wyman's full line of berry products is also available to the foodservice trade throughout the U.S. and Canada via the Wyman brand and distributor labels. And the company continues to serve the industrial trade. Wyman's supplies many of America's best muffin and pie bakeries and has customers ranging from prominent yogurt and jam brands in Japan to Maine's own premier jam maker — Stonewall Kitchens.

But what makes Wyman's special is not just the Barrens, the most fertile wild blueberry fields in the world. It is the people of Wyman's. From the Wyman family through management, to the farm, factory and office staff and the growers who supply Wyman's, all abide by the core principle of "continuous improvement" of everything Wyman's does. As a result, in 2012 Wyman's met the expectations of the GFSI (Global Food Safety Initiative) by receiving SQF (Safe-Quality-Foods) certification. Wyman's is also a top performer on SYSCO's Sustainable Farm Audit and is a proud member of the Sustainable Food Lab and The Pollinator Partnership.

Wyman's holds itself to the standards set forth in its Sustainability Mission and places equal priority on the triple bottom line of economic profitability, environmental stewardship and social equity. A prime example of Wyman's commitment to its Sustainability Mission is its national leadership role in seeking a solution to the mysterious die-off of honeybees, known as Colony Collapse Disorder.

As a responsible farm, important rural employer, and global supplier, Wyman's has been proud to call itself a Maine company for over 140 years and looks forward to the challenges and successes of the next 140.

General Dynamics Bath Iron Works

PHOTO COURTESY OF GENERAL DYNAMICS BATH IRON WORKS (G. BRIDGMAN)

Located approximately 15 miles from the open ocean, BIW is a modern, full-service shipyard occupying approximately 58 acres on the west bank of the Kennebec River. BIW has built ships on this site since its founding in 1884. In 2001, the Land Level Transfer Facility, seen in the foreground of this picture, was inaugurated, providing BIW with a more flexible and efficient way to build ships.

Proudly continuing Maine's 400-year shipbuilding heritage, the men and women of BIW build the finest destroyers afloat for the US Navy.

General Dynamics Bath Iron Works (BIW) is the recognized leader in the design, construction and lifetime support of the world's most technologically advanced surface combatant ships operated by the U.S. Navy. Today, from its modern shipyard on the shores of the Kennebec River, the men and women of BIW proudly continue a local shipbuilding heritage that stretches back over 400 years.

Shipbuilding in this region began at the mouth of the Kennebec River, just a few miles south of BIW's current location. In 1607, the settlers of the Popham Colony launched a 50-foot, oceangoing sailing ship named Virginia, the first ship built by Europeans on this continent. In the 18th and 19th centuries, Bath, Maine was a shipbuilding center known worldwide as the "City of Ships," a moniker still claimed by its citizens.

Bath Iron Works was incorporated at its current site in 1884, just as wooden ships and sails were giving way to iron, steel, and steam engines. Capitalizing on these new technologies, BIW quickly built a reputation for quality and innovation in ships of all types and sizes, including cargo and passenger ships, luxurious yachts, and warships. Since its founding, BIW has constructed more than 245 military ships and over 160 private yachts and commercial vessels.

During World War II BIW honed its expertise in warship construction, building more than 80 ships that accounted for 20 percent of all destroyers delivered to the U.S. Navy. At its peak rate of production, with a workforce of 12,000 men and women, BIW delivered a new destroyer to the Navy every 17 days.

Since 1995, BIW has been part of General Dynamics, a market leader in business aviation; combat vehicles, weapons systems and munitions; shipbuilding and marine systems; and mission-critical information systems and technology.

BIW has long been a landmark for travelers along the Maine coast and an economic force throughout Maine, especially in the Midcoast region. To residents and visitors alike the shipyard's towering cranes signal arrival in Bath from coastal U.S. Route 1.

With over 5,000 employees and an annual payroll of more than $320 million, BIW is the largest single site manufacturing employer in Maine. Additionally, the business BIW conducts with other companies in Maine injects over $50 million annually into the state's economy.

BIW's skilled workforce includes professionals in manufacturing trades, management, engineering, planning, and many other areas. The majority of BIW employees come from Maine, where shipbuilding roots run very deep. In some cases, BIW ships are being built today by fourth or fifth-generation family members, and it is common to find several members of the same family working at the shipyard. Overall, its employees average over 20 years of shipbuilding experience.

BIW's experienced workforce is complemented by a modern shipyard facility that reflects recent capital investments of over $400 million. Inaugurated in 2001,

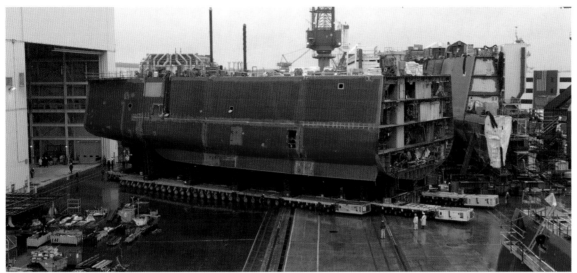

the Land Level Transfer Facility is where ships are built, launched and retrieved using any one of three shipbuilding stations. This facility, coupled with a new, environmentally controlled Ultra Hall assembly building, has led to many BIW process improvements that are revolutionizing the way naval surface combatants are built. Driven by a focus on continuous improvement, BIW delivers unprecedented productivity, legendary quality, and affordability.

Naval warship construction is a highly complex undertaking given the size and technological sophistication of the final product. For example, a typical Arleigh Burke (DDG 51) class guided missile destroyer is 510 feet long, weighs 9,300 tons and contains 6,200 tons of steel, nearly 50 miles of piping, over 250 miles of electrical cable, 6,500 light fixtures, and thousands of mechanical and electronic pieces of equipment

BIW builds ships in large modules which can weigh up to 5,000 tons, more than twice the weight of a World War II destroyer. Modules are assembled, painted and outfitted within environmentally controlled buildings which provide a safer, more comfortable and more efficient work environment. When each module is complete, it is then transported outdoors onto the Land Level Transfer Facility where it will be joined with other modules. When the ship reaches a high level of completion, it is moved into a drydock and floated off for final systems activation and testing. When it goes to sea for the first time, BIW employees operate the ship through a series of rigorous tests and demonstrations known as "sea trials" to prove its quality and performance to the Navy customer. A successful sea trial leads to the delivery of the ship to the Navy and its ultimate welcoming into the fleet at its commissioning ceremony.

Since 1991, BIW has delivered 34 Arleigh Burke class destroyers to the U.S. Navy. After a DDG 51 ship built by BIW or another shipyard joins the fleet, BIW provides design and engineering support to the Navy for modernization and maintenance throughout the ship's 35 – 40 year life span. BIW's eight home port offices around the world provide services for these ships wherever they are deployed.

BIW is proud to be building three of the U.S. Navy's newest and most technologically advanced ships, the

Zumwalt (DDG 1000) class destroyer. These ships, the first all-new destroyers designed for the U.S. Navy in many decades, contain many new technologies, including an advanced electric drive propulsion system, a wave-piercing hull form, composite superstructure, advanced radars, and extensive automation, providing reduced crew size and lower operating costs. As these ships enter service over the next few years, they will deliver revolutionary capabilities to the U.S. Navy.

Above all, BIW's core business is the design and construction of complex naval surface combatants and, as a full-service shipyard, it also specializes in the design and manufacture of highly outfitted, complex assemblies. The company's workforce is focused on customer satisfaction and possesses considerable experience in collaborating with contractors, suppliers, and other groups.

Beyond business, BIW employees have a proud record of community involvement. Whether supporting the United Way, food drives, fundraisers, or construction of Habitat for Humanity homes, BIW employees are engaged.

Since 1884, BIW has consistently demonstrated how to build tough, high-quality and affordable ships. Innovation and constant improvement are the underpinnings of its continuous pursuit of greater efficiency and value to its customers and shareholders. BIW is a company steeped in heritage, ready for the future and proud to be in Maine.

Top: An "Ultra Unit" for the future *USS Zumwalt* (DDG 1000) is transported from the Ultra Hall (white building on left) onto the Land Level Transfer Facility to be joined with another module. Weighing more than 4,000 tons, this was the largest ship module ever moved at BIW.

Bottom: *Michael Murphy* (DDG 112) on sea trials in the Gulf of Maine. DDG 112 is the 34th Arleigh Burke class AEGIS Destroyer built by BIW. The ship is named for LT Michael Murphy, USN, a US Navy SEAL killed in action in Afghanistan in 2005. For his actions, he posthumously received the Medal of Honor.

Bath Built is Best Built: The legendary performance of BIW's battle-tested US Navy destroyers and today's unyielding commitment to innovation, quality and affordability give BIW a reputation that is second to none.

Maine Academy of Natural Sciences at Good Will- Hinckley

Maine Academy of Natural Sciences is located on the 1,700 acre Good Will-Hinckley campus in Fairfield, Maine.

Maine Academy of Natural Sciences at Good Will- Hinckley is an educational program of its parent organization, Good Will-Hinckley, named for George Walter Hinckley, who founded The Good Will Home for Boys and Girls in 1889. Since its founding in 1889, Good Will-Hinckley's mission has been to provide a home and schooling for youth who are "in need of a helping hand." The organization has fulfilled this mission in different ways over the years and continues to abide by it now through its different programs.

Today that commitment is best expressed with its partnership with the Maine Academy of Natural Sciences, MeANS. The school opened in September 2011 as a private magnet school focused on serving at-risk students through the themes of agriculture, forestry and sustainability. MeANS provides an inspiring and inclusive learning environment primarily for students who are under-engaged and at risk of dropping out of high school. The school serves day students from the central Maine region and boarding students from across the state who are looking for alternatives to traditional schools. In fall 2012 MeANS will operate as Maine's first public charter school.

MeANS has developed a contemporary mission focused on today's learner and building the skills he or she needs in order to succeed in today's workforce — and in life. What hasn't changed since Good Will-Hinckley's

MeANS is the first high school in Maine to focus on agriculture, sustainability, forestry, workforce skills training and independent living.

founding in 1889 is the organization's commitment to meaningful student-teacher relationships, real-world learning experiences, and its ties to the land.

With the hundreds of acres of the Good Will-Hinckley campus in Fairfield, Maine, serving as its outdoor classroom, MeANS utilizes Hinckley's inherent attributes through project-based experiences and individualized learning. Using Individualized Learning Plans, MeANS students are actively involved in mastering the Maine Learning Results, Common Core Standards and other unique MeANS graduation goals, using an innovative curriculum grounded in the themes of forestry, agriculture, and the environment. This curriculum is taught by experienced teachers with both subject matter expertise and skills with at-risk populations.

The curriculum is designed to provide students with multiple pathways to graduation by utilizing an individualized, hands-on, project-based approach to learning. A typical school day for a MeANS student is anything but typical. The format includes two hours of classroom instruction; two hours of elective activity/job shadowing, internships, or coursework at Kennebec Valley Community College; and two and a half hours of individual and group project work.

Examples of group projects include building raised beds in the greenhouse, researching and planting cover crops on a large garden plot to feed students living in cottages, or mapping out forest inventory growth plots

for each student in the woods. Individual projects can range from researching the history of G.W. Hinckley by contacting alumni and reading primary source materials; studying the feasibility of keeping five baby mice alive after losing their mother; building a gravity-fed, rain water-based watering system for the greenhouse; or building bridges in swampy areas of the forest trails.

For the residential student, the campus has a number of dorm cottages staffed by experienced Campus Living Advisors. Campus Living Advisors provide coaching in a specific curriculum of independent living skills. Proficiency and mastery of these skills is necessary to meet graduation standards.

"Core values of the academy are respect, responsibility, and service to the community," says the school's co-director, Emanuel Pariser.

Students at the Maine Academy of Natural Sciences are encouraged to re-engage with their education and complete their education with more self-direction. One of the goals for the students is to grow as critical thinkers and problem solvers by developing habits of heart and mind that lead them to take responsibility for their own actions, as well as for the welfare of other students, their community and their environment.

MeANS also plans to play an increasingly important role in its community in relation to food and nutrition issues, supporting projects to feed the homeless and hungry, as well as teaching neighbors effective ways to grow food that will sustain them through times of low and under-employment.

MeANS also has plans to serve as an educational hub for the natural sciences, working with local elementary, middle and high schools to provide on-site visits, workshops, and lesson plans that local teachers can use to encourage agriculture and forestry projects in their own districts.

"Our intent is to work in partnership with the public schools in this state. We understand how hard they work with this student population and we want to reach out to them and collaborate on developing the most successful educational path for students who may require an alternative to the traditional classroom," says Dr. Glenn Cummings, who accepted the position of President and Executive Director of Good Will-Hinckley in 2010 after serving in President Barack Obama's administration as Deputy Assistant Secretary for the U.S. Department of Education.

The school's campus will also soon be home to Kennebec Valley Community College, giving MeANS students an introduction to college life and access to college-level courses, including the state's only Associate Degree in Agricultural Sciences.

Other goals set by MeANS are to significantly broaden and establish its internship and apprenticeship offerings, diversify and expand its fundraising base, and offer year-round courses and a co-curricular schedule.

With seemingly limitless opportunities for on-campus, outdoor learning, MeANS will continue to offer more and more types of in-depth, project-based lesson plans that tap into these resources, whether they be in the forests, the river, using alternative energy, or cultivating new crops.

Based on the above enrollment projections and the careful, systematic build-out of its educational program, by the year 2020 the school expects to have graduated several classes of students who will go on to post-secondary success at college, work, and in their communities.

MeANS teachers and students working together on a hands-on learning project.

Our mission is to graduate actively-engaged students who are proficient in all graduation standards, have completed at least one college-level course, and have used the community and the natural world as their classroom.

Maine Eye Center

Maine Eye Center's physicians: back row, from left, Jeffrey K. Moore, M.D., Richard A. Bazarian, M.D., F.A.C.S., Peter S. Hedstrom, M.D., Frank W. Read, M.D., Frederick S. Miller, M.D., Curtis M. Libby, M.D., Natan D. Kahn, M.D.; front row, from left, Charles M. Zacks, M.D., Jeffrey L. Berman, M.D., R. Samuel Cady, M.D.

With a practice lineage of over 100 years, Maine Eye Center embraces its role as Northern New England's most comprehensive eye specialty practice.

Maine Eye Center began with the practice of one doctor, Sylvester "Judd" Beech, M.D., in 1907. Thirty-nine years later, ophthalmologist Richard Goduti, M.D., joined the practice, which he later took over when Dr. Beech retired. Frank W. Read, M.D., partnered with Dr. Goduti in 1971 when the company was known as Ophthalmology Associates, until its name was changed in the early 1990s to Maine Eye Center. With Dr. Read's leadership, the practice has grown steadily over the past 41 years. By adding new doctors, new locations, and using advanced technology, Maine Eye Center continues to grow and provide expert care to the people of Maine and New Hampshire.

Today Maine Eye Center has grown to 10 ophthalmologists and four optometrists practicing at two Maine locations — the Lowell Street campus and the Stroudwater Crossing campus in Portland.

Maine Eye Center is the most comprehensive eye care private practice in Northern New England. Specialties include cataract and anterior segment surgery, retinal and vitreous diseases and surgery, ophthalmic plastic, lacrimal and orbital surgery, corneal and external diseases and surgery, iLASIK™ and refractive surgery, pediatric ophthalmology, adult strabismus, glaucoma management and surgery, and routine optometric eye care and contact lenses.

In addition, Maine Eye Center is partnered with

Maine Medical Center to exclusively provide all of its ophthalmic emergency services.

In January 1987, Maine Eye Center became the first medical practice in the state of Maine to have a Medicare Certified Ambulatory Surgical Center. Since that time, Maine Eye Center has performed tens of thousands of surgical procedures at its facility, which allows patients to undergo outpatient surgery without going into the hospital.

Dr. Libby is the head physician of LaserVision, a division of Maine Eye Center, which offers state-of-the-art refractive surgery. By using the Advanced CustomVue™ process and the IntraLase™ bladeless method, MEC is able to customize the iLASIK™ procedure for each patient.

At MEC's Stroudwater Crossing location, Dr. Kahn serves as the head of the Eyelid Surgery Center. Dr. Kahn performs endoscopic and direct browlifts, blepharoplasty, lacrimal and orbital surgery.

As the lead physician of Maine Eye Center's Pediatric Center, Dr. Berman provides diagnostic consultations and medical and surgical management of children's eye disorders, as well as adolescent eye disorders. The pediatric eye care staff offers care for children's common eye problems as well as comprehensive evaluations.

The retina doctors at Maine Eye Center, Dr. Bazarian, Dr. Miller, Dr. Hedstrom, and Dr. Moore, have

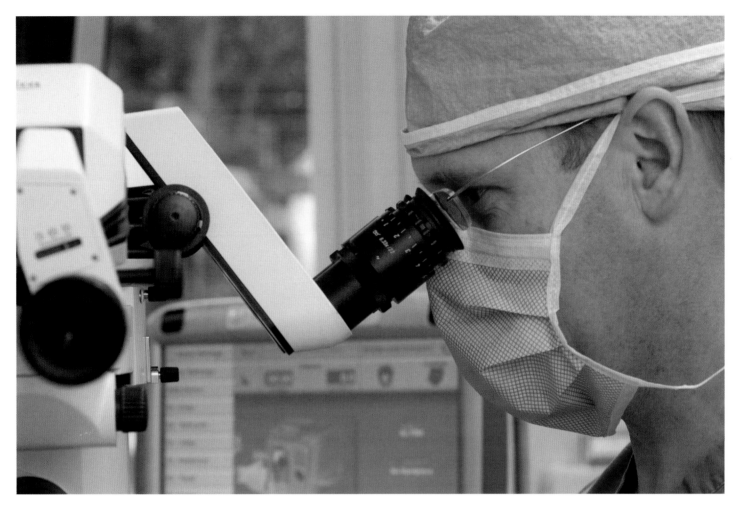

had special training in treating retinal conditions and diseases. They take great care to diagnose and treat problems and diseases of the retina, including macular degeneration, diabetic retinopathy and retinal detachment.

The team of cataract physicians and surgeons of the Cataract Center is comprised of Dr. Cady, Dr. Hedstrom, Dr. Libby, Dr. Read, and Dr. Zacks. Until recently, most lenses implanted after the removal of the cataract were monofocal implants that generally provided good distance vision, but glasses were still necessary for optimum near vision. Now with advances in lens technology, many patients can expect to see well at near, far or intermediate distances with less dependence on glasses after their cataract surgery.

Dr. Zacks, a fellowship-trained ophthalmologist specializing in medical and surgical management of corneal and external diseases of the eye, serves as the head of MEC's Cornea Center. Keeping the cornea healthy is a vital part in protecting your vision and the health of your eyes. Whether you need contact lenses for keratoconus, treatment for acute corneal problems or cornea transplant surgery, Dr. Zacks and his team can help.

Glaucoma is the second leading cause of vision loss. Dr. Cady and Dr. Libby in the Glaucoma Center help manage and attempt to slow the progression of glaucoma. While there is no cure, early detection, careful monitoring, the use of certain medications and procedures can slow progression of the disease and reduce the risk of vision loss.

MEC's four optometrists, Dr. Aggarwal, Dr. Amundson, Dr. Thees, and Dr. Walters, provide routine eye care for all ages. For those with stable vision and without known eye disease, having routine eye exams every two years is important to maintain health vision.

For many years Maine Eye Center has been offering the services of an optical shop to its patients and to the public. MEC has two optical shops staffed by opticians certified by the American Board of Opticianry carrying a wide variety of economy and designer eyeglasses, sunglasses, and accessories.

The staff at MEC is actively involved in the communities it serves. For example, MEC has been a sponsor of the Portland Based Iris Network's White Cane Walk to help sustain services for people who are blind or visually impaired. MEC employees raise donations and participate as a team known as "Eyes on a Cure" in Portland's Making Strides Against Breast Cancer program.

The practice holds a monthly Jeans Day, where employees donate $2.00 or more to wear jeans to work. Each month's donations support a different charity, such as the Preble Street Resource Center, the Barbara Bush Children's Hospital, and the Good Shepherd Food Bank. Additionally, many of the doctors and staff participate in international relief organizations such as Project Guatemala and cureblindness.org.

Most of all, the Maine Eye Center staff enjoys helping the people of Maine and Northern New England to see the world around them and to better enjoy all of life's little details.

Medicare Certified Ambulatory Surgical Center

"When you do a cataract operation on a grandmother, and she comes back the next day and tells you she just saw her grandchild for the first time in five years, that's when you know why you do it," says Frank Read, M.D.

Farm Credit of Maine

Chief Executive Officer and President Ray Nowak spends time with new employees at the Auburn office to discuss Farm Credit's unique lending and technology partnerships, both at the state level and within the national Farm Credit System.

"In many respects, the way we conduct business is a direct reflection of the traditional industries we are chartered to serve," says Ray Nowak.

Since 1916, Farm Credit of Maine has been recognized as a steady and reliable lender by Maine's traditional natural resource-based industries. A state-wide credit cooperative, Farm Credit of Maine is part of the 96-year old Farm Credit System, which today holds approximately $230 billion in total assets and is the largest provider of agricultural credit in the U.S.

In addition to its long history of financial stability, this very specialized, customer-owned lending institution has grown steadily for nearly 100 years, always rising to the challenge as the need increases for financial capital to run modern small and larger-scale natural resource-based businesses.

Farm Credit of Maine operates under a limited federal charter with a focus on Maine's natural resource-based industries — agriculture and food, commercial fishing and seafood, forest products — and rural communities.

Farm Credit provides its customers in the agriculture and food industry with working capital loans to finance livestock, seed, chemicals and fertilizer; real estate loans for land purchases and production facilities; and commercial loans to finance new equipment, consolidate debt, or manage business when faced with adverse industry conditions. And it partners with state-sponsored training programs whose curricula are designed to help entrepreneurs and owners of small and traditional and non-traditional natural resource businesses.

There are many ways Farm Credit loans and related services help commercial fishing customers. All along the New England coast, Farm Credit actively participates in industry fishing and seafood tradeshows. For many years, Farm Credit has offered support to Maine's working waterfront programs to help ensure access for Maine's fishermen.

Farm Credit's customers in the forest products industry benefit significantly from flexible loan structuring options for land, buildings, equipment, and working capital. Farm Credit actively participates in industry associations whose members include loggers, foresters and small woodlot owners, and it contributes to forestry education programs that help prepare people for careers in the forest products industry and create public awareness about Maine's sustainable forestry practices.

From mortgages to commercial loans, Farm Credit supports its rural property customers through lending against commercial and residential value, and it offers competitive interest rates and terms as well as local servicing.

Farm Credit of Maine functions as an independent cooperative. That means when someone receives financing or services, he or she becomes a Farm Credit customer-owner. Customer-owners elect a board of directors from among the membership. "This traditional cooperative governance structure has a way of keeping

us all focused on serving our customer-owners with the right blend of efficient modern banking technology — and a highly personal touch," says Chief Executive Officer and President Ray Nowak.

In addition to delivering services with a personal touch, Farm Credit loan officers make it their business to understand industry cycles and offer flexible terms that reflect seasonal needs and match business cash flows. Decision-making rests at a local level. Farm Credit uses a traditional "relationship lending" model — where a customer's loan officer will handle the transaction from the first "hello" to beyond the closing.

All Farm Credit business is transacted with the convenience of rural-based family businesses in mind. Farm Credit's lenders are often on the road, meeting their customers throughout all of rural Maine — on the farm, in the woods, or on the waterfront. "This not only saves time and expense for our customers, but it also keeps us in tune with the day-to-day challenges and rewards of running a business in rural Maine," says Chief Lending Officer Fred Morton, a Farm Credit employee for over 30 years.

While Farm Credit's focus is always on the best loan structure for its customers, it's not only about lending. In response to customer need, Farm Credit offers related services through its carefully chosen business partners that provide leasing and crop insurance. Farm Credit's licensed appraisers provide professional commercial and rural property appraisals.

Denver-based CoBank, which is also an independent cooperative and federally chartered for wholesale and retail lending, is an important Farm Credit of

Maine partner and the primary funding source for the Maine cooperative. CoBank is the largest institution within the national cooperative Farm Credit System. "The combination of a financially strong wholesale lender like CoBank and a financially strong retail lender like us, plus the fact that we are both owned by our customers, makes for an efficient, focused, and stable banking business model. It's simply a great way to do business," says Nowak.

This way of doing business even returns profits to the customer-owners of the cooperative. Every year since 1996 Farm Credit of Maine has consistently shared its profits with its members through patronage distributions totaling more than $26 million.

"At the core of everything we do," says Nowak, "it's still about people."

Farm Credit customers are served and supported by a dedicated staff of professionals, many holding lengthy tenures at the company. It is not uncommon for employees to retire from Farm Credit having worked there for more than 25-30 years. "As employees, we know that traditional natural resource industries are the economic and social foundation of rural Maine, and we're proud to be helping with the success of these businesses so rural Maine can prosper and the state's strong and diverse rural heritage and values can live on well into the future" says Dick Robertson, Chief Risk Officer and a 39-year Farm Credit employee.

Combine industry and banking expertise with the traditional cooperative principals that keep the customer as the focal point for everything, add some mobile technology and some unique partnerships, and it's a recipe for success — for nearly 100 years.

Farm Credit's office in Presque Isle serves members and rural communities in Maine's northern region – Aroostook County and parts of Penobscot and Washington counties.

Farm Credit of Maine has built its success on a firm foundation: a solid mix of industry and banking expertise, traditional cooperative principles, mobile technology, unique partnerships – and the belief that the customer should be the focal point of every service and every decision.

Mercy Health System of Maine

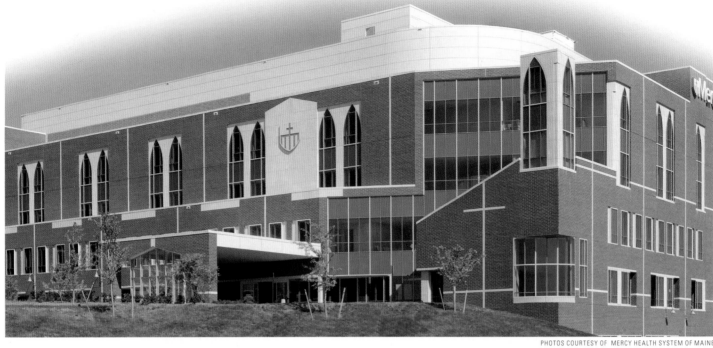

Mercy's Fore River campus opened in 2008 along the beautiful Fore River in Portland.

Mercy has always been about more than just bricks and mortar and high-tech advances. Since its founding in 1918, the organization remains true to its core value: compassion and respect for the dignity of every human being, in a setting of spiritual support.

Mercy is a comprehensive provider network that administers physical and behavioral health care services and is a member of Catholic Health East, a multi-institutional Catholic health system serving communities through regional health care systems in 11 eastern states from Maine to Florida. Its mission is to carry out the healing work of Christ by providing clinically excellent, compassionate health care for all, with special concern for the poor and disadvantaged.

Mercy has played an integral role in caring for the people of the greater Portland community since the hospital's founding nearly 100 years ago. It began in response to the deadly influenza pandemic of 1918 that claimed the lives of more than 5,000 Mainers and more than 50 million worldwide.

In response to this severe and deadly health care crisis, the Sisters of Mercy, a Catholic religious order with 60 active nuns living and working in Portland at the time, mobilized to staff the Marion Weeks Mansion located at 681 Congress Street. Miss Weeks had previously given her residence to the Roman Catholic Diocese of Portland in order to provide space to care for the many local victims of the flu. Bishop Louis S. Walsh, then the leader of the Portland Catholic Community, dedicated the building as "Queens Hospital," and it was quickly renovated and equipped to care for 25 women patients.

As the patient census at Queen's Hospital steadily grew, additional buildings were added to meet the need. In 1933, with the introduction of Blue Cross pre-paid health insurance, the need for additional space became imperative. In response, hospital staff and trustees began formulating plans for a new hospital building. A ladies' Auxiliary also was established, with civic-minded members of the greater Portland community contribut-

ing their time and talent to Mercy's mission. Today the Mercy Auxiliary remains an active partner in assisting the hospital achieve its goals through its members' philanthropic and volunteer efforts.

Recognizing the need for someone to shepherd the hospital through a major transition of growth and into the future, the trustees appointed Sister Mary Annunciata Quigley as its first administrator. And in 1943, the new 150-bed Mercy Hospital opened at 144 State Street in Portland.

Today, the Mercy System includes the state's leading in-patient substance abuse and treatment center (the Mercy Recovery Center at Westbrook) Mercy Fore River, the short-stay hospital on the banks of the Fore River which opened in 2008; VNA Home Health Hospice; and its original building on State Street. As of 2012, the Mercy Health System employs more than 2,000 and is a major economic driver in the region.

In the tradition of the Sisters of Mercy and in keeping with its role as a community hospital, Mercy has continued to reshape itself to the needs of its patients while striving to meet the highest quality and value standards. This effort includes bringing heath care to patients through responsive community-based services. It also involves a continuous refining of systems to reduce inpatient stays and hasten recovery times through careful patient education and a highly focused pre-operative regimen.

Mercy's clinically excellent and compassionate care is underscored by a long list of "firsts and only," including: Portland's only hyperbaric oxygen chambers for wound healing; one of the only hospitals in Maine with surgeons dedicated only to breast surgery; the only health care organization north of Connecticut with a disease-specific Joint Commission certification in Spine; the first cochlear implants to be performed in the State of Maine;

Each year, Mercy provides in excess of $10 million in community benefits and care for the poor, including charity care, pro-bono services, community education, and prevention outreach.

Maine's first and only hospital to receive the Governor's Award for Business Excellence; and the exclusive health care provider for the Maine Red Claws.

In recent years, Mercy has evolved into a health care provider increasingly dedicated to outpatient services, and it has built an extensive Primary and Express Care network to bring care where people live.

Primary Care facilities now exist in Yarmouth, Portland, Windham, Standish, Westbrook, Gorham, Falmouth, and Falmouth. Four Express Care Practices are located in Gorham, Westbrook, Windham, and Yarmouth and are open seven days a week from 8:00 am to 8:00 pm. They are a convenient and low cost alternative to using the Emergency Room.

Mercy's network of Specialty Providers includes Addiction Medicine, Cardiology, Eating Disorders, Gastroenterology, Hematology/Oncology, Otolaryngology (ENT), Pulmonology, Wound Healing, Breast Care, Diabetes, Food & Ankle Orthopaedics, General Surgery, Obstetrics/Gynecology, Pain (Medical & Interventional), and Urology/Urogynecology.

The Orthopaedic Institute at Mercy, a partnership with the Southern Maine Orthopaedic Management Company, is a regional leader in physician-led, quality patient outcomes. With this partnership, 23 Orthopaedic Surgeons from 7 separate practices cover the spectrum of orthopaedic specialties, including total joint replacement, sports medicine, foot and ankle surgery, spine surgery, hand surgery, orthopaedic trauma, and pediatric orthopaedics. Mercy has earned The Joint Commission's Gold Seal of Approval™ in disease-specific certification for its Hip and Knee Replacement Program as well as a disease-specific certification in Spine.

Mercy, however, has always been about more than just bricks and mortar and high-tech advances. Since its founding in 1918, the organization remains true to its core value: compassion and respect for the dignity of every human being, in a setting of spiritual support.

This commitment is embodied not only in the care provided to each patient, but also in how Mercy gives back to the greater Portland community. One example

is Mercy's Gary's House, a "home away from home" for families of patients at any area hospital who cannot afford prolonged stays at a hotel when a loved one is seriously ill or injured; and McAuley Residence, a transitional housing program for women and their children.

Each year, Mercy provides in excess of $10 million in community benefits and care for the poor, including charity care, pro-bono services, community education, and prevention outreach. The comprehensive diabetes education offered through The Mattina R. Proctor Diabetes Center at Mercy is just one example of this benefit.

For nearly a century, Mercy has filled a unique niche in greater Portland's health care community. In today's uncertain world, Mercy's commitment continues to provide the care needed, where it's needed.

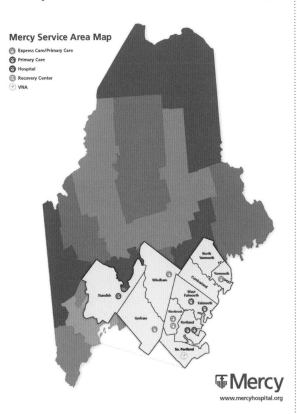

Above: Dr. John Devlin consults with a patient at Mercy's Mattina R. Proctor Diabetes Center.

Below: Mercy's extensive network of hospital, primary, express, and specialty care locations brings health care where people live throughout Southern Maine.

Maine State Credit Union

The main branch of Maine State Credit Union was built in 2000 and occupied in 2001. Prior to 2001, teller services, loan services and the administration offices were housed in different buildings. Combining departments into one location improved efficiency and service.

"Our technology has changed, our size has changed, but our values haven't," says Normand Dubreuil, CCUE, CCE; president and CEO.

Maine State Credit Union was organized in October 1935 by state employees for the purpose of providing small loans to fellow state workers in times of emergency. According to the original by-laws, "The purpose of this credit union is to promote thrift among its members, by affording them the opportunity for accumulating their savings, and to create for them a source of credit for loans for provident and productive purposes." This original purpose has never been altered.

When the credit union began, it took only twenty-five cents to join and a fully paid share was five dollars. Membership was limited to employees located in the State House building and their immediate families.

In 1944, the enactment of the Credit Union Law made it possible for the credit union to convert from a federal to a state credit union. With this change in the charter, the credit union became known as Maine State Employees' Credit Union, and at that time, the charter was broadened to include all state employees as potential members.

In 2004, the Credit Union was granted a community charter for Kennebec County, making anyone who lives, works, worships, or attends school in Kennebec County eligible for membership. At the beginning of 2005, Maine State Employees' Credit Union changed its name to Maine State Credit Union.

In 2006, Greater Waterville Area Federal Credit Union merged with Maine State Credit Union to become the Greater Waterville Area Branch of Maine State Credit Union, which also expanded its membership to include Somerset County.

From its humble beginnings beneath a stairwell in the state house building 77 years ago, Maine State Credit Union has since become the largest credit union in Maine with seventy-one employees, $340 million in assets, over 25,000 members, and three branches: two in Augusta and one in Waterville.

An account at Maine State Credit Union is much more than just a number and a place to put a paycheck. An account at the credit union means being a part owner of the credit union. Unlike a bank, there are no highly paid stockholders at the top of the food chain. Any profit made above the credit union's expenses goes back to the member. The credit union's board of directors is formed by volunteers that are elected directly from its membership.

Becoming a member of Maine State Credit Union is easy. The following people are eligible to join Maine State Credit Union: anyone who lives, works, worships, or attends school in Kennebec County or Somerset County; Maine state employees; employees of the Maine State Employees' Association; Cumberland County employees; Maine Housing Authority Employees; members of the Maine Association of Retirees; employees of the Maine Technical College System; Maine State Retirement System employees; retirees of any of the preceding groups listed here; and any individual who is receiving a Maine State retirement pension, and their immediate family or household members.

Maine State Credit Union prides itself in offering outstanding service to its members and continues to embrace the core values of offering diverse products. The credit union offers a robust range of products, including savings and checking accounts, share certificates (CD's), money market, club accounts, individual retirement accounts, health savings account, and coverdell IRAs. For its younger members, the credit union offers a youth savings program, Monty Moose Youth Savings Program, the Credit Union Succeed Teen Club and the Free4ME checking account.

The pooling of resources to provide loans is one of the keystones of the credit union movement. Though that pool of resources has gotten much bigger and more complicated, Maine State Credit Union's loans are made in the same co-operative way they were in 1935. As a credit union, its members are a group of people helping others in the community get the credit they need while keeping every member's financial resources secure.

Maine State Credit Union offers a full range of lending products and Visa credit cards to meet its members, financing needs, including fuel, auto, home and personal loans, home equity loans and lines of credit, pre-approved loan drafts and overdraft protection loans.

In addition, the credit union has always made service its priority. Maine State Credit Union offers a variety of options to help its members get their banking done when they want, how they want. Options include online banking and bill pay, CUe Statements, Touch Tone Teller, shared branching locations and SURF network ATMs, eAlerts! and MSCU Mobile.

Maine State Credit Union is committed to being a socially responsible organization in the communities in which its members live and work. The credit union values improving its community through involvement in fundraising, volunteering and general concern, and creating a positive image through community efforts and the commitment and dedication of its employees to social responsibility. In 2007, Maine State Credit Union won the Dora Maxwell Award for Outstanding Achievement in a Social Responsibility Program.

Each year, Maine State Credit Union supports over 40 community organizations and causes dedicated to improving its community. These organizations help support youth growth and development, education, financial education, healthcare, nutrition and fitness, sports and athletics, personal development, ending hunger, ending homelessness, advancements in technology, arts, culture and music, and many more. Maine State Credit Union also awards twenty $1,000 scholarships to graduating high school seniors each year.

The credit union is an avid supporter of the Maine Credit Unions' Campaign to End Hunger. Maine State Credit Union has been the top fundraiser for the Campaign to End Hunger every year from 2006 to 2011, and it was the first credit union in Maine to raise over $40,000 in one year for the Maine Credit Unions' Campaign to End Hunger. Through fundraising efforts supporting the elimination of hunger in Maine, Maine State Credit Union has raised over $250,000 to date. Throughout the year the credit union holds a number of fundraisers, including the annual Walk to Stop Hunger in the spring and the spaghetti dinner and auction in the fall.

Maine State Credit Union has been a champion of Ending Hunger in Maine for 13 years. In that time over $250,000 have been raised in large part by the annual Walk to Stop Hunger held at Capitol Park in Augusta. Here Normand Dubreuil, CCUE, CCE, president and CEO of Maine State Credit Union cuts the ribbon with Linda Johnson, from Spectrum Generations, as they begin the annual Walk to Stop Hunger

From its humble beginnings beneath a stairwell in the state house building 77 years ago, Maine State Credit Union has since become the largest credit union in Maine.

Anthem Blue Cross and Blue Shield in Maine

PHOTO BY BRIAN FITZGERALD | FITZGERALD PHOTO

Anthem volunteers build raised beds at the Maine Veterans' Home in Scarborough during Anthem's annual Community Service Day, when Anthem associates contribute their time and energy to help local community organizations.

The long heritage of Anthem in Maine includes serving all of the state's 16 counties with a broad range of products, programs and services that help keep Maine families healthy. Anthem's mission: to improve the lives of the people it serves and the health of its communities.

In 1938 Maine's first health insurer was founded to provide Mainers with security around their health care needs. Today, Anthem Blue Cross and Blue Shield in Maine still provides that essential security, combining its local roots with the national strength of its parent company, WellPoint, Inc. to provide coverage options to Maine individuals, seniors and employers of all sizes. "Our long heritage in Maine includes serving all of our state's counties with a broad range of products, programs and services," noted Dan Corcoran, president and general manager of Anthem. "While we're thought of primarily as a health benefits company, we're also a major local employer with hundreds of Maine-based associates in good jobs."

Relying on innovative data-driven approaches to improving quality, Anthem applies an integrated approach to improving health that engages members, health care providers and employers to help members make good decisions about their health needs. Anthem uses its extensive local health care data to develop information that supports doctors at the point of care and provides critical insights into the health of populations. The company's toolkit includes personalized information that engages members in staying well, managing illness and saving money; incentives that support providers in keeping their patients well and managing their illnesses; and technology that improves communication and decision-making.

In a groundbreaking use of intelligent technology, Anthem will be offering doctors the ability to use Watson, the "Jeopardy!"-winning computer, to outline treatment options and diagnoses. Watson will meld the latest medical research, population health information,

and the patient's own medical history and lab results and analyze millions of pages of data in seconds to help doctors make better decisions, faster.

Because research shows that the right financial incentives coupled with the right support tools result in better outcomes and lower costs, Anthem rewards health care providers for coordinated care focused on disease management, wellness, prevention, quality and safety. For example, Anthem's participation in the Patient Centered Medical Home initiative represents a fundamental shift in how an insurer interacts with primary care doctors on all levels: clinically, contractually and operationally. Members gain coordination across the continuum of care and a focus on wellness and prevention. The primary care doctors gain greater collaboration with their patients, an enhanced ability to manage their patients' health, and the ability to succeed in an environment that recognizes and rewards higher quality care. Over time, the Patient Centered Medical Home initiative is expected to result in improved health outcomes at a lower cost.

Anthem's new MyHealth Advantage program identifies opportunities for Anthem members to improve their health by sending individualized messages to members and their doctors about needed services, such as missed screenings and prescription refills. Another Anthem program, Availity®, helps local physician practices reduce time-intensive administrative tasks related to benefits and payments. And the Availity CareProfile®, a patient care record that includes information from doctors, pharmacies, labs and other providers of care can play an important role in improving quality, safety and efficiency.

130   MAINE — A PHOTO PORTRAIT OF THE PINE TREE STATE

PROFILES IN EXCELLENCE

PHOTO BY COREY TEMPLETON

PHOTO COURTESY OF MAINE WINTER SPORTS CENTER

The Anthem Blue Cross and Blue Shield Foundation provides significant funding to support programs that add to the health and wellbeing of Maine people in key areas measured by Anthem's State Health Index.

A nthem's longtime presence in Maine has resulted in a powerful culture of supporting local communities. In addition to local giving, the Anthem Blue Cross and Blue Shield Foundation supports a variety of critical programs and services that promote the health and wellbeing of Mainers.

"In support of our mission, the majority of our charitable support is aimed at health-related causes," said Corcoran. "Using our State Health Index as a guide, our efforts focus on some of Maine's most pressing health issues." Anthem's State Health Index, developed from information collected by the Centers for Disease Control and Prevention (CDC), continually tracks eight guiding measures of public health focusing on maternity and prenatal care, preventive care, lifestyle, illness and death.

To help Maine address the predicted shortage of trained nurses in the future, Anthem's foundation provided funding for the Anthem Blue Cross and Blue Shield Foundation Nursing Simulation Center at Central Maine Community College, which enables nursing students to gain valuable clinical experience in a state-of-the-art laboratory where nursing students can train on lifelike patient simulators. A similar grant funded Northern Maine Community College's Allied Health Simulation Laboratory, which trains nursing and EMT students in the northern part of the state.

In its ongoing efforts to encourage healthy lifestyles, Anthem joins with a range of organizations to reach out to children, families, adults, seniors and the workforce with support that helps improve their health. These include YMCAs throughout Maine, which hold the YMCA's Healthy Kids Day to show children and families that they can enjoy staying active; the Schoodic Education and Research Center Institute for the Healthy Kids for a Healthy Acadia program, which targets grade school-aged and preteen children in Washington, Hancock and Aroostook counties who are at risk to become overweight; the OASIS Institute, which trains adults age 50 and older to teach the CATCH (Coordinated Approach to Child Health) Healthy Habits program to children in kindergarten through fifth grade; and the Boys & Girls Clubs, where kids in Maine joined their peers across the nation to break the Guinness World Record for the most people doing jumping jacks at one time.

In addition to the company's strong commitment to corporate philanthropy, Anthem associates have a long history of supporting community causes, from events on the South Portland campus that raise funds for a broad range of causes to Anthem's Associate Giving Campaign, which in 2011 donated over $173,000 to agencies across Maine. "We're proud to be a company made up of Maine people who care deeply about the state where we live and work," said Corcoran.

Top: A major grant from the Anthem Foundation improved the popular Back Cove section of the Portland Trails system. Funding helped enhance trail safety for thousands of Mainers who use the trail each year for running, walking, and biking.

Bottom: Anthem helped showcase world-class athletes as primary sponsor of the E.On IBU Biathlon World Cup hosted by the Maine Winter Sports Center in Presque Isle and Fort Kent. The economic boost to Aroostook County included showing 120 million TV viewers the quality of life in northern Maine.

Pratt-Abbott Drycleaners

The company's free home and office pickup and delivery is a big hit with today's busy customers.

Pratt-Abbott Drycleaners is a family-owned business that has served the Portland community since 1944.

When a middle-aged woman walked into the Forest Avenue Pratt-Abbott carrying a decades-old wedding dress, she doubted it could be restored to its former splendor. Both her mother and grandmother had said their vows in it this dress. Now her daughter hoped to wear it in her upcoming nuptials. Pratt-Abbott manager Laurie Basinet was determined to make it happen.

While not as old as the wedding dress, Pratt-Abbott Drycleaners has been a family business serving the Portland community since 1944. The business started out as a solitary store in Bramhall Square at a time when over 20 different drycleaners plied their trade in Maine's largest city. Although Pratt left the business a year after its founding, Elliot Abbott became the face of the company for 14 years, often waiting on customers and pressing shirts himself.

Abbott opened up new stores and diversified to meet demand. In the 1940s he combated unemployment by hiring veterans through the GI Bill. One of these hires was Rodrick Lowell, an ambitious WWII vet who worked his way from the shirt presses to taking over ownership of the company in 1958 when Abbott retired.

The alterations and tailoring department boomed as more women entered the work force and had less time to mend their own clothes. When the masses moved to the suburbs, Pratt-Abbott followed suit, opening branches in Portland's outlying communities. Over the decades, Pratt-Abbott has continued to meet evolving customer needs by opening laundromats, launching a uniform

rental division, and creating a free home pickup and delivery service that lets customers avoid special trips to drop off or pick up their clothes. The company has also adopted sustainable practices such as using recycled materials for packaging and creating drop-off stations for recycling hangers and garment plastic.

Through all these changes, Pratt-Abbott's greatest asset continues to be the people behind the company. In an increasingly impersonal world, Pratt-Abbott has maintained a community feel. "We're part of the neighborhood," Sue Cairns states of the Westbrook store where she has worked for over 30 years. "I've been here so long that the kids of long-time customers are now customers."

Terry Talbot, who worked at the Westgate store for 25 years before retiring, says, "I miss joking around with the customers the most. When I retired, I got so many cards and letters from the regulars. It was really touching."

Laurie Basinet loves seeing the smile of a satisfied customer. Her favorite tasks to work on are those that carry sentimental value to people. She personally consulted with the mother of the bride on the best way to treat the antique wedding dress and the potential risks. After soaking and pressing the garment herself, Laurie was thrilled to tell the customer that it had been restored.

This commitment to quality is universal to Pratt-Abbott employees. Basinet says of her co-workers, "The people here are outstanding. My crew will jump in wherever needed. It's a team effort."

Today, Pratt-Abbott, Maine Cleaners and Pratt-Abbott

uniform employ over 150 Mainers, making it the largest dry cleaning company in northern New England. Most of the stores serve as drop-off and pick-up locations. The Forest Avenue and South Portland stores double as plants where the clothes for every store and home delivery route are cleaned and pressed. The main office in Westbrook houses the plant for the uniform division.

From the beginning, Pratt-Abbott has been a family business. The Abbott family still takes their dry-cleaning to the Forest Avenue store. Rod and the Lowell daughters were frequent presences behind the counter. Rod's father, Adrian Lowell, worked on the machinery in the Westbrook coin-op until his late eighties.

In 1991, the Lowells sold the business to the father and son team, Jim and David Machesney. Since then, Machesney children and grandchildren have helped man counters, drive vans, and bag shirts for Pratt-Abbott. Although Jim has retired, David runs 13 stores under the Pratt-Abbott/Maine Cleaners name along with the constantly expanding uniform rental department.

Dave is a third-generation drycleaner. He represents the industry on regional and national trade boards. Closer to home, his community support extends to a number of organizations.

To Pratt-Abbott, being part of the community goes beyond providing service to their patrons. The stores with reader board signs use the space to publicize local events and fundraisers — from blood drives to high school sporting events. Pratt-Abbott supports the Portland art scene by cleaning costumes for several theater companies free of charge. Most notably, Pratt-Abbott is a major sponsor of two charities that benefit Maine's underprivileged youth: the Salvation Army and Camp Susan Curtis.

The Coats for Kids program provides gently used winter coats for impoverished Mainers. Together with the Salvation Army, Pratt-Abbott launched the program in 1983 after noticing that many families couldn't afford expensive jackets that their children would soon outgrow. Each year, Pratt-Abbott cleans all of the coats donated for free.

Terry Talbot says that from her 25 years at Pratt-Abbott, she is most proud of how much Coats for Kids has grown. Back when it started, all of the coats were cleaned in the Westgate coin-op. "Customers used to ask why I was cleaning all these kids jackets," Terry says, "The next week they'd come back with jackets their kids had outgrown."

Today, Coats for Kids is well known throughout Maine. It collects over 26,000 coats each year for both children and adults. Pratt-Abbott employees often volunteer extra time to help sort and clean all of the coats.

In 2007 Pratt-Abbott began its partnership with Camp Susan Curtis, a tuition-free summer camp for disadvantaged Maine children. Pratt-Abbott cleans and delivers the laundry of every camper and counselor free of charge. This lowers costs for the camp, allowing more children to attend. At Camp Susan Curtis, campers learn life skills while enjoying traditional camp activities. Melissa Cilley, the camp's Executive Director, states, "Beyond the skills and asset development, the children of Camp Susan Curtis also have their basic needs met, sometimes for the first time. And, thanks to Pratt-Abbott, they have clean clothes. This service is a tremendous gift to the children we serve."

For nearly four generations, Pratt-Abbott's commitment has been deeply woven into the very fabric of their business. Whether this means a pristinely pressed bridal dress for a wedding, a meaningful place for employment, or a warm coat on a child's back, the company continues to make a positive impact in the Maine com-

Left: Exceptional care of clothing and customers have always been hallmarks of Pratt-Abbott, as shown in this 1956 photo.

Right: Pratt-Abbott picks up the tab for cleaning the clothes of every camper and counselor at Camp Susan Curtis, so every attendee can focus on having fun.

Over the decades, Pratt-Abbott has continued to meet evolving customer needs by opening laundromats, launching a uniform rental division, and creating a free home and office pickup and delivery service.

Washington County Community College

Paula Cleaves from Perry, a Business Management graduate, at WCCC's 2012 graduation ceremony.

Washington County Community College helps people to discover choices and create success.

The smallest of Maine's seven community colleges, Washington County Community College (WCCC) is located in Calais, on the border with New Brunswick, Canada. The Maine Legislature created the college in 1969 as Washington County Vocational Technical Institute, with the first classes held in the Calais Armory. The following year, the college moved to its present location in Calais on 400 acres overlooking the St. Croix River. In 1986, the Maine Vocational Technical Institute System was established by the Legislature, and three years later the name of the college was changed to Washington County Technical College.

A major turning point in the college's history occurred in 1993 when the New England Association of Schools and Colleges, through the Commission of Technical and Career Institutions, extended the accreditation status of the college from a non-degree-granting institution to an associate's degree-granting institution. That same year, St. Croix Hall, which houses a gymnasium, small auditorium and the Culinary Arts program, was completed.

In 1999, the college was authorized by the Maine Technical College Board to offer the Associate in Arts in Liberal Studies, thereby expanding its mission to prepare students for transfer to baccalaureate programs. In 2003, by act of the 121st Legislature, the Maine Technical College System became the Maine Community College System and WCTC was renamed the Washington County Community College.

WCCC has been recognized in 2011 and 2012 by the prestigious Aspen Institute for being in the top 120 community colleges in the nation. The college is grounded in a sound philosophy of student success and uses this strength to build a capable work force for Washington County and Maine. Over the years the campus has seen numerous improvements, including the recent completion of a new student center and library, and renovations to a number of existing classrooms.

The college offers 24 associate degrees, diplomas and certificates in various technical and career fields from medical assisting and welding to automotive technology and education. WCCC has a number of program transfer agreements with four-year institutions throughout Maine to assist students with transfer upon meeting the necessary course requirements.

A wide range of credit and non-credit courses are also offered in the evening, during the summer term, and through the internet. Programs are designed to provide the technical knowledge and skills as well as the essential general education with which to pursue a career after graduation. The Liberal Studies program offers students the opportunity to obtain the first two years of a baccalaureate credential at WCCC before transferring to another college or university.

The Certificate credential is an important part of the success of students because it offers an achievable one-year completion goal. Many certificates are "stackable," students have the opportunity to gain skills in one occupational area and return to study for a second year in a related occupational area to become multi-skilled technicians and earn an associate's degree. Technical and career programs provide classroom instruction in theory, and students practice skills in laboratories or in clinical training sites. Modern classrooms, laboratories and training areas are the site of caring, student-centered instruction. Students also have the opportunity to pursue a transfer degree in liberal studies.

Application-based learning in real life settings is the hallmark of instruction at WCCC. It is common for students to complete community service projects reflective of the objectives of their training. For example, building construction students, trained in renovation and assisted by the residential and commercial electricity students, may help build a new office at the local police department. Heavy equipment operations students extend their skills by completing important earthwork for the Moosehorn Wildlife Refuge.

Students have the opportunity to live in apartment-style housing and study in a multicultural, international environment. Canada and two tribes of Passamaquoddy people bring a richness of diversity that few campuses enjoy.

Located in the housing complex is the Outdoor Adventure Center, which provides all types of equipment from tents and mountain bikes to skates and kayaks, as well as a climbing wall in the St. Croix Hall gymnasium. Along with serving adults, the Center brings in many K-12 students to use the climbing wall or to learn to hike and kayak, helping the public and private schools to meet guidelines on student wellness and environmental awareness.

Maine's ruggedness and geographic diversity, from the ocean to the mountains, provide many opportunities for outdoor adventures and sports activities, from fly fishing for salmon in Grand Lake Stream to snowmobile and ATV excursions on well-groomed trails. The College, located adjacent to the historic St. Croix River, also abuts Moosehorn Wildlife Refuge with its many hiking and cross-country ski trails and opportunities to study wildlife. In addition, the beauty of the region inspires the work of many artists, musicians and writers who come to Washington County to work or study.

WCCC serves as an educational, community, and economic development resource for Washington County and beyond by providing educational opportunities with individualized attention to all who desire to gain technical skills, develop career specializations, engage in self-improvement, and/or prepare for transfer.

Hillary Holbrook, a heavy equipment maintenance student, participates in a live training at the Moosehorn Wildlife Refuge.

Harvard Pilgrim Health Care

Harvard Pilgrim Maine office staff: top row, from left, Jon Edwards, John Baumer, Carolyn Preston, Patrick Denning, Ed Kane, Tony Fournier; bottom row, from left, Danielle Campbell, Steve Conley, Nicole Fairweather, Jessica Bineau, Callie Lubinski.

Harvard Pilgrim is Maine's only local, not-for-profit health plan, and it is recognized across the country for outstanding quality and customer service.

Harvard Pilgrim is driven by a passion for making health care work better for the people and communities it serves. With the goal of improving value and quality across the health care system, Harvard Pilgrim collaborates with consumers, doctors, employers and brokers to offer innovative and customized solutions delivered with exceptional service.

Harvard Pilgrim is Maine's only local, not-for-profit health plan, and it is recognized across the country for outstanding quality and customer service. For a number of years it has been consistently named the #1 private health plan among the nation's best health plans by the National Committee for Quality Assurance.*

For employer-customers, and their employees and families, Harvard Pilgrim offers a wide range of coverage options. Its consumer-driven health plans with health savings and health reimbursement accounts encourage members to get preventive care and think carefully about how they spend their health care dollars. Easy-to-use retiree plans are available not only to employers, but to individual customers as well. Also, Healthy Futures, Harvard Pilgrim's groundbreaking incentive-based program for improving employee wellness, rewards members for taking steps to improve their health.

Throughout Maine, Massachusetts and New Hampshire, Harvard Pilgrim's extensive network includes doctors and hospitals that members know and trust. When employees live and work in different parts of the country, employers can turn to Harvard Pilgrim for national coverage solutions through an al-

liance with UnitedHealthcare.

Harvard Pilgrim has long been recognized for its leadership and innovation in prevention and disease management. Whether it's through online tools or working directly with a personal health coach, Harvard Pilgrim provides the necessary resources to help members make healthier lifestyle decisions. Harvard Pilgrim's care management programs and dedicated nurse care managers also help members deal with conditions such as asthma, diabetes, coronary artery disease or other complex conditions to help minimize complications and improve their well-being.

Through Harvard Pilgrim's Quality Grants program, physician practices in Maine, Massachusetts and New Hampshire received close to $1 million in 2011 to fund initiatives that support the patient-centered medical home concept. This emerging care delivery model encourages partnerships between patients and primary care physicians to help achieve better health outcomes.

In the patient-centered medical home approach, care teams attend to the multifaceted needs of patients and provide "whole person," comprehensive and coordinated patient-centered care. The needs and desires of patients come first in an environment where patients have collaborative relationships with their primary care physicians and care team.

In Maine, four provider groups — Quality Counts in Augusta; St. Mary's Regional Medical Center in Lewiston; Maine Medical Center PHO in Portland; and Nova-Health, LLC in Yarmouth — have received grants from Harvard Pilgrim for initiatives that focus on one or more aspects of care coordination, which is a critical component of the patient-centered medical home model of care.

Grant recipients have an opportunity to transform how primary care practices operate and to drive improvements that can positively impact not only Harvard Pilgrim members, but also all of their patients. The results of the grant programs are shared with other Harvard Pilgrim providers at regular meetings so that "best practices" can benefit a broader patient population.

The Harvard Pilgrim Health Care Foundation provides the tools, training and leadership to help build healthy communities. Since its inception more than 30 years ago, the Foundation has awarded more than $100 million to programs that support healthy eating and active living for children and families, enrich local schools, care for the homeless, clean the environment and make health care more equitable.

In fact, in 2011 alone, the Foundation awarded more than $1.3 million in grants to almost 1,000 not-for-profit organizations in Maine, Massachusetts and New Hampshire. Of Harvard Pilgrim's 1,100 employees, 98% participated in some form of giving through volunteering, the Community Spirit 9/11 Mini-Grants program, and the annual employee fundraising campaign. In Maine, more than $9,000 in mini-grants was distributed to non-profit organizations in communities throughout the state.

As part of the Foundation's 30th anniversary celebration, Harvard Pilgrim employees chose to donate $10,000 to Camp Sunshine in Casco. Over the years, many Harvard Pilgrim employees have also volunteered for service days at Camp Sunshine to help get the camp ready for the hundreds of children with life-threatening illnesses and their families who visit free of charge each summer.

Additionally, The Foundation's Growing Up Healthy initiative supports programs that help prevent childhood obesity. Working with the Let's Go! 5-2-1-0 Goes to School program, more than 112,000 elementary school-aged children ate better and moved more through grants to 21 schools in Greater Portland and Somerset and York Counties, as well as through training for local school nutrition directors.

The Foundation's Culture InSight program will also help 20 Maine communities better prepare to serve minority and immigrant populations through the launch of the Hanley Center's Health Leadership Development Alumni Ambassador Program in Portland. The program will implement projects across the state with a primary focus on reducing health disparities.

Harvard Pilgrim further supports its mission — to improve the quality and value of health care for the people and communities it serves — with participation on state government committees and sponsorship of key community events.

* NCQA's Private Health Insurance Plan Rankings, 2011-12 HMO/POS. NCQA's Health Insurance Plan Rankings 2010-11 – Private. U.S.News/NCQA America's Bests Health Insurance Plans 2005-2009 (annual). America's Best Health Insurance Plans is a trademark of U.S.News & World Report. NCQA The State of Health Care Quality 2004.

The Harvard Pilgrim Health Care Foundation provides the tools, training and leadership to help build healthy communities.

Harvard Pilgrim employees at an annual Service Day at Camp Sunshine in Casco.

IDEXX Laboratories

The IDEXX Laboratories world campus in Westbrook.

Keeping animals healthy, milk and water safe through the development and manufacture of innovative diagnostics and information-sharing products and services.

IDEXX Laboratories was founded by David Shaw in 1983 with five employees in the Old Port neighborhood of Portland, Maine to respond to a new niche market, the detection of diseases in livestock and poultry animals such as cows, pigs and chickens. Within a few years, the company distinguished itself as a leader in immunoassay kits, including the now industry-renowned SNAP® family of tests that detect diseases in cats, dogs and other animals. By 1991, IDEXX had become a publicly traded company and over the next 25 years grew to become a world leader in veterinary diagnostic instrument development and manufacture; reference laboratory services; and dairy and water testing. Put simply, the company keeps animals healthy, milk and water safe.

For instance, when thousands of pets were left homeless in Japan after a devastating tsunami in 2011, IDEXX Laboratories provided testing that ensured the health and safety of cats and dogs throughout the region. After most of the Boston metro area water supply was compromised by a main break in 2010, IDEXX tests were used to determine if public water was safe to drink.

And before chicken, pork, beef or even milk are placed on your dinner table, IDEXX tests and health monitoring systems for livestock and poultry may have ensured productivity and safety, and contributed to your peace of mind.

In addition to providing diagnostic testing products, IDEXX is committed to helping veterinary practices thrive by supporting change and continuous improvement through advanced information-sharing technology, education and knowledge. This is accomplished through proprietary practice management systems and education channels such as the IDEXX Learning Center. In 2011, IDEXX also introduced pethealthnetwork.com, a trusted resource where veterinarians can connect with pet owners seeking to learn more about keeping pets healthy and happy.

Today, the company headquarters are located in Westbrook, where it continues to thrive. Since 2002, the employee population in Maine has doubled under the leadership of CEO Jonathan Ayers, with two major expansions involving an investment of $80 million in local facilities undertaken since 2006. IDEXX's workforce is now more than 5,000 strong worldwide with one-third of its employees based in southern Maine. And in 2008, the company surpassed the $1 billion revenue mark just 25 years after start-up.

In 2011, IDEXX invested $76 million in research and development, most of which occurs at the Westbrook headquarters, resulting in products that are exported

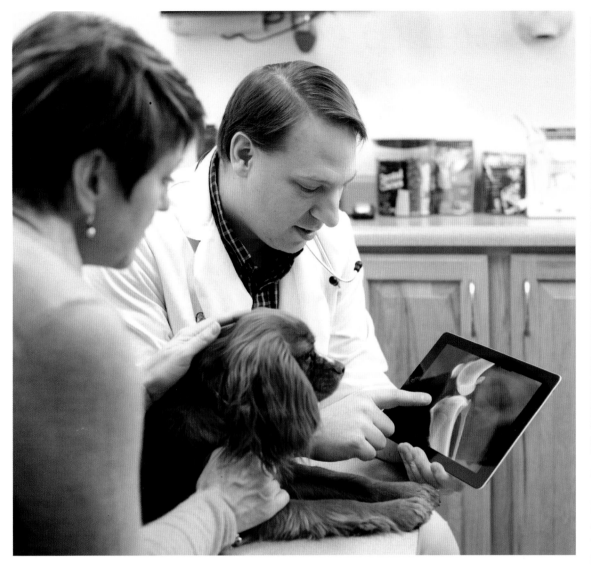

The purpose of IDEXX is to be a great company that creates exceptional long-term value for its customers, employees and shareholders by enhancing the health and well-being of pets, people and livestock.

Jake Zaidel, DVM, uses IDEXX I-Vision Mobile™ app for efficient, portable digital imaging — providing real-time care through innovation.

to more than 100 countries around the globe. IDEXX's purpose is to enhance the health and well-being of pets, people and livestock, and the company accomplishes its mission through intelligent innovation that produces a steady stream of new products and services.

But IDEXX isn't just science and engineering. The Maine facilities comprise the company's global headquarters and primary manufacturing and research and development centers. For that reason, career paths for Maine employees include sales and marketing, manufacturing, information technology, finance, legal, human resources, administration and other specialties.

IDEXX employees worldwide are also committed to Guiding Principles that shape how they approach their day-to-day work: achieve and sustain market leadership; exceed the expectations of our customers; empower and reward our employees; innovate with intelligence; cultivate entrepreneurial spirit; and contribute to our communities.

Through the recently launched Global IDEXX Volunteer Efforts (GiVE) program, all full- and part-time IDEXX employees are given two paid work days each year to contribute to their communities. This program has resulted in tens of thousands of volunteer hours to benefit a myriad of causes, with as many as 25,000 vol-

unteer hours in Maine annually. Additionally, IDEXX contributes financially to a number of organizations in Maine, including United Way, Animal Refuge League of Greater Portland, Gulf of Maine Research Institute, Maine Center for Creativity, Portland Symphony Orchestra and Maine educational systems such as the Maine Community College Foundation and the University of Maine system.

IDEXX takes sustainability seriously through an approach that aligns with business objectives, ensures social and stakeholder responsibility, and demonstrates environmental stewardship. In 2012, IDEXX was honored with the Governor's Award for Environmental Excellence for its accomplishments in making sustainability a key factor in various business decisions the company has made since 2008. The company also began construction in 2012 on Westbrook's first LEED® certified building, a new administrative facility that will expand its world campus.

In keeping with IDEXX's commitment to fostering employee well-being, the company espouses both mental and physical health through a significant employee health and wellness center slated for opening in 2013; the introduction of a new collaborative workspace design that is being adopted as a best practice by other highly innovative companies; and a focus on serving healthy meals in the multiple on-site cafeterias.

Acadia Insurance

Acadia Insurance office on County Road in Westbrook

Acadia Insurance was founded April 2, 1992 in response to the Workers' Compensation crisis in Maine to provide insurance to local businesses throughout the state. Its first office was located in South Portland with approximately 60 employees. As the business quickly expanded, Acadia relocated to its current location on County Road in Westbrook. Today, Acadia employs over 200 people in Maine, and another 150+ people in offices located throughout the Northeast.

The declaration page of the first policy written still hangs in the amphitheater of the Westbrook office – a reminder of the company's beginning only 20 years ago.

Charlie Hamblen, Chief Financial Officer of Acadia Insurance, has been with the company since its inception.

"Maine was a great place to start an insurance company in the 90s, and not that many people realized it," says Hamblen. "Most insurance companies had left the state and left us with a pool of talented people, a committed independent agency force and many policyholders looking for a local, customer-oriented insurance company that was financially stable. The first account that we wrote in 1992, we still write today."

Acadia has been propelled by the vision and belief that local businesses want a local insurance carrier with a hands-on approach to service. This means being located in the states in which it operates, and employing people in the communities it insures so the compa-

Businesses choose Acadia because of its dedication to excellence and expertise in the insurance field.

ny can provide responsive service and local expertise. This continues to be Acadia's differentiating value to its customers.

The key to Acadia's 20 years of success in the insurance industry has been knowledge of its local markets, focus on commercial insurance, and a steadfast commitment to working in close collaboration with its agent and association partnerships. "This local model embodies our vision of 'closer coverage.' We feel a strong sense of responsibility to provide the best insurance solution to the customers in the communities we operate because these are our communities, too," says Doug Nelson, president of Acadia Insurance.

Fifteen employees who were part of Acadia's first year still work at the company today, like Steve Rich, vice president of claims." Acadia has provided me with the opportunity to work with many committed employees over the years, delivering superior service to our customers, while impacting our company results each and every day," says Rich.

Employees at Acadia believe in the company's vision, which can be witnessed in the commitment to delivering excellent service to its customers. Businesses choose Acadia because of its dedication to excellence and expertise in the insurance field.

Expanding from one office located in Maine, Acadia now has additional offices in Connecticut, Massachusetts, New Hampshire, New York and Vermont.

Acadia provides targeted insurance solutions to small and mid-size businesses, in the areas of property, general liability, workers compensation, commercial auto, and umbrella.

In addition, Acadia has a specialty division of Inland and Ocean Marine professionals who can provide businesses with tailored insurance products for their marine exposures including businesses involved in construction, transportation, warehousing, jewelry, antiques and fine arts, and business and personal watercraft.

Acadia Insurance works exclusively through a network of select independent agencies to deliver its insurance products and services. The company believes that independent agents provide invaluable insurance expertise to help business owners make the best decisions for their business. The independent agents are part of their local communities, and as fellow business members, they understand the individual needs of their customers. For that reason, Acadia chooses to work exclusively through a network of over 200 agencies located throughout the Northeast.

Entrepreneurial spirit is an intangible quality that has persisted in Acadia Insurance since its founding. It can be seen in Acadia's vision statement as well as its employees' dedication to excellence. Part of it also is a commitment to "do the right thing."

"Doing the right thing means doing what is right for the customer, even if it makes our jobs more difficult. It means being resourceful and exploring all possible solutions if a problem arises," said Rich. "Our customers and agents know that they can count on us to do what is right. And that is one of the best ways that we can serve our local communities."

Acadia Insurance serves the local community in other ways as well. Each year, Acadia Insurance donates thousands of dollars to local charities in each of the states in which it operates. For Maine, the list includes organizations like the Ronald McDonald House and Dress for Success in Portland. Employees at each office form a committee and select charities or organizations to donate funds that benefit the local community. Acadia focuses on charities and organizations that provide job and skill development, art enrichment, or health and well-being education programs.

In addition to monetary giving, Acadia employees are also actively involved in their local communities by donating their time to organizations like the Preble Street Soup Kitchen, United Way and Habitat for Humanity. Since 2008, Acadia employees have given over 2,750 hours of their time to serving local communities. Also during that time, Acadia has donated a percentage of its annual income to charitable organizations throughout New England and New York that meet its contribution guidelines.

Acadia Insurance is a member of the W. R. Berkley Corporation (NYSE: WRB), a Fortune 500 Company that is one of the nation's premier commercial lines of property casualty insurance providers and one of the 50 largest diversified financial companies in the United States. W.R. Berkley Corporation is rated A+ (Superior) by A.M. Best for financial strength.

Doug Nelson, president, Acadia Insurance

"Our customers and agents know that they can count on us to do what is right. And, that is one of the best ways that we can serve our local communities," says Vice President of Claims Steve Rich.

The MEMIC Group

The MEMIC Group's corporate office located in the historic Old Port area in Portland.

"Our philosophy has remained intact for the past two decades — to make workplace safety our mission and to treat injured employees with the best and most effective treatment available," says President and CEO John T. Leonard.

Portland-based The MEMIC Group, headed by Maine Employers' Mutual Insurance Company, is a workers' compensation insurance company that began as the guaranteed insurer for the employers in Maine and has since grown into a strong regional company with its sights set on even more growth.

When it began as a private mutual insurer in January 1993, few believed that the company would survive its first few years, let alone become a foundation of the state's business economy. But over the last 20 years, that's exactly what has happened.

At its formation, the company set out to be a different kind of insurer, and its laser-like focus on injury prevention was the basis for that vision. As such, MEMIC's founders stressed the creation of an environment where employers and employees would work together to help reduce injuries. This required a change in workplace culture to place a high value on workplace safety. This action would ultimately help to control costs and keep jobs from fleeing the company's home state.

MEMIC focused on working with its 20,000 policyholders and their 200,000 employees to create safer workplaces through regular training in the best safety practices available. The company began this effort with the creation of a MEMIC department, which hired people directly from the industries they would serve to act as safety consultants and trainers. In addition, the company launched the "Partnership for Workplace Safety" public awareness campaign which emphasized workplace safety as prominent value in every Maine workplace. In recent years, the company has created innovative ways to help educate policyholders about workplace safety

through online methods, including exclusive webinars and a web portal known as MEMIC Safety Director.

To say that philosophy has worked would be an understatement. Since MEMIC's formation in 1993, lost-time injuries in Maine have been reduced by nearly 40 percent, and the overall cost of workers' compensation insurance in the state has been reduced by nearly 50 percent. By working to resolve disputes between employers and employees and by assuring appropriate medical care for injured workers, the company has become a leader in the area of injury management. In a competitive market where there are nearly 200 insurance companies licensed in Maine, MEMIC has remained the leader, insuring approximately 60 percent of Maine's commercially insured employers.

"We opened for business nearly 20 years ago and our philosophy has remained intact for the past two decades — to make workplace safety our mission and to treat injured employees with the best and most effective treatment available," says John T. Leonard, president and CEO since the company's inception in 1993. "These are tenets that help to reduce the cost of insurance and maintain a healthy relationship within the workplace. Our innovative programs in safety and claim management are the ingredients that lead to customer retention which approaches record levels for our industry."

As a result of its success in Maine, the company attracted attention across the country, which helped it to grow strategically beyond Maine. Today, The MEMIC Group includes the original company plus two insurance subsidiaries. Together, the group is licensed to write workers' compensation in 45 states plus the Dis-

PHOTO BY RICHARD SANDIFER

trict of Columbia. It has been among the top five workers' compensation insurers in New England for the past five years and is among the fastest growing insurers in the mid-Atlantic.

The company actively markets its products throughout the northeast. In addition to its headquarters in Portland, the company has offices in Manchester, New Hampshire; Glastonbury, Connecticut; Albany, New York; Weehawken, New Jersey and West Conshohocken, Pennsylvania. The company's assets are approaching $1 billion. MEMIC is rated A (Excellent) by A.M. Best and has earned accolades across the industry for its efforts in technology and customer service.

"The MEMIC way is spreading down the Eastern Seaboard," Leonard said. "Everywhere we go, we find

that our focus on workplace safety and superior claims service is important to employers. It's exciting and gratifying to see that our efforts pay off as we export our business model."

Back home in Maine, the company remains a pillar of the local business community and has received countless awards for its efforts in economic development, business leadership, social responsibility, ethical leadership and, of course, workplace safety.

The MEMIC Harvey Picker Horizon Scholarship is awarded annually to the child of an injured worker whose family's ability to pay for college has been significantly impacted by the worker's injury. To date, the company has made scholarship awards totaling nearly $100,000.

Membership organizations include the Greater Portland Chamber, Maine Chamber of Commerce, the New England Council, Maine Businesses for Sustainability, and the Safety and Health Council of Northern New England. MEMIC is also a member of national insurance trade organizations which help to foster good public policy that serves its policyholders.

Employees at MEMIC are also involved members of their local communities. MEMIC encourages this involvement by example and by getting behind efforts to raise funds and help local communities. Chief among these efforts is its annual United Way campaign. Annually, MEMIC's employees pledge more than $50,000 to the local United Way. In addition, employees have led efforts to raise funds for organizations such as the local chapter of the American Heart Association, the National Kidney Foundation, the Red Cross and many others. Employees in the home office in Portland raise thousands of dollars each year for "Strike Out Cancer in Kids," a fundraiser for the Maine Children's Cancer Program.

MEMIC believes in fair treatment and honest dealings in all that it does, whether with employees, policyholders, injured workers, agents, regulators, vendors or other business partners.

Mainebiz

Members of the Mainebiz editorial team, from left, Staff Writer Matt Dodge, Senior Writer Jim McCarthy, Online Editor Mindy Woerter and Editor Carol Coultas, far right, discuss a cover design with Graphic Designer Matt Selva.

The mission of Mainebiz is to be the leading source of Maine business news and analysis.

Mainebiz is a multimedia company providing business news, information and analysis for business owners and C-level executives in Maine. Founded in 1994, with offices in Portland, Mainebiz delivers Maine's business news and information in a variety of ways to help the statewide business community access what it needs: online, in person at events, and in multiple media such as print, social media, video and enewsletters.

Mainebiz covers business and economic trends, issues and news through credible, evocative and stimulating writing; consistently produces high quality, well-designed products with exceptional art, graphics and photography on issues critical to the business community; and provides a forum for ideas for Maine's business community.

In 1994, John Whitney, a Maine native who had launched a number of specialty newspapers in Maine, had just returned from Boston where he had started a retail guide for Newbury Street and a neighborhood paper for Cambridge. He returned to Maine to pursue the idea of a creating a new business journal.

With about $1,500 in startup money, Whitney produced his prototype. "It was a totally bootstrap operation, but it was always a serious business journal," says Whitney.

By 1999 the paper had expanded beyond Portland, was published every other week, and had professional staff in each department. Annual ad revenues approached $400,000. Balancing the desire to continue growing the business with the need for more cash flow, Whitney sold Mainebiz that year to Worcester Publishing Co., now called New England Business Media, the parent company of Worcester Business Journal and Hartford Business Journal.

Today, Mainebiz reports revenues upwards of $1.9 million and delivers Maine's business news not only through its bi-weekly print publication, but also via daily emails, an interactive website, social media, videos, data, supplements, directories, and numerous events for the business community throughout the year.

Mainebiz excels at its commitment to providing opportunities for members of Maine's business community to come together. For example, the Mainebiz Momentum Convention is an annual event produced for Maine's business community. The Augusta-based convention brings together CEOs, marketing executives, human resources managers, business owners, sales managers, technology directors and professionals to spend a day with their peers learning, networking and getting inspired to build momentum for their business. Companies can exhibit their products and services in the large Exhibition Hall, while advancing skills and learning best practices at the Mainebiz U educational sessions. The convention provides many networking opportunities throughout the day, culminating with a reception on the floor of the Exhibition Hall.

Mainebiz produces three annual events to honor and recognize successful business leaders. These include the Mainebiz Business Leaders of the Year, where

three Maine business leaders who demonstrate their leadership and business acumen are selected for the annual award. Nominees are considered from three categories: a large company of 50 or more employees, a small company of fewer than 50 employees, and a nonprofit organization.

Each year *Mainebiz* honors exceptional executives selected from a pool of nominations for the Women to Watch recognition. Honorees are business owners, CEOs, presidents and top executives who have a proven track record of success, who are trailblazers and mentors.

Another signature recognition is The Next List, which identifies 10 future leaders of Maine's business community. Nexters have demonstrated leadership, entrepreneurship, positive relationships within the community, business savvy, and are key to the state's economic future.

In addition, *Mainebiz* also produces several supplements and directories for the Maine business community. Supplemental publications include The Fact Book, data and statistics collected from many sources that provide the business community with a clear picture of the Maine marketplace. It answers questions such as, "Where are the growth areas in Maine?," and, "How competitive are the municipal tax rates?"

Mainebiz researches companies, executives and transactions in many industries and ranks them by various factors in its annual Book of Lists. The Book

of Lists data is in high demand, and can also be purchased as Excel files online.

Mainebiz is honored to be the recipient of multiple national, regional and local awards for its journalistic excellence and outstanding design and graphics. *Mainebiz* belongs to the national Alliance of Area Business Publications and has won the AABP "Best Paper" award from 2004-2009, and has earned a "Best Overall Design" award every year since 2004. The company has also won awards from the New England Press Association, including first place for General Excellence in 2007. Most recently, *Mainebiz* received a Best of Business award from the Society of Business Editors and Writers.

Mainebiz demonstrates its commitment to the community by consistently supporting the arts, charities and business organizations as a company and as individuals, through in-kind donations, monetary donations and volunteer hours. In addition, the company established the *Mainebiz* Next List Alumni Scholarship Fund via the Maine Community Foundation to benefit a Maine college student who is majoring in business.

"There is never a lack of interesting stories to tell about the business community of Maine, " says Publisher Donna Brassard. "Businesses in Maine are creative, adaptable and proactive. There is a pervasive sense of entrepreneurship here that complements the state's unique resources, and a deep commitment to preserving the excellent quality of life we all share."

Members of the Mainebiz advertising, marketing and audience development departments discuss customer service. From left are Donna Brassard, publisher; Betsy VanderPloeg, senior accounts manager; Jenna Grant, events/marketing manager; Julianna Myers, audience development marketing specialist; Leila Musacchio, advertising director; and Ken Hanson, senior accounts manager.

"Our quality products, dedication to customer service and ability to be flexible, innovative and proactive has helped us to be a profitable media business that is, in fact, growing," says Donna Brassard.

Casco Bay Steel Structures, Inc.

Fabrication bay, Saco facility.

"Our primary goal is 100% customer satisfaction," says Bryon Tait.

asco Bay Steel Structures is a prime example of a how hard work and an unwavering commitment to producing an excellent product makes for a winning combination. After years of experience in the industry, Bryon Tait, and his wife Wendy, who handles the financial side of the business, founded Casco Bay Steel Structures in 1997. The company fabricates structural steel for bridge construction and transports the bridge girders to bridge-building sites throughout New England and New York.

In its first year of business, the South Portland-based company had three employees, and has since then grown exponentially over the past 15 years. The company now employs 75 people and has a 55,000 square foot steel processing plant in Saco and a newly-opened, state-of-the-art assembly plant of 100,000 square feet in South Portland, resulting in facility space totaling approximately 155,000 square feet, with 100 tons of lifting capacity over 30 acres of property. The South Portland plant hosted an official ribbon-cutting ceremony last summer when the new facility opened. With the additional space now available to accommodate the massive steel girders, the company is now able to handle multiple jobs and go after bigger projects.

The company competes with a handful of large, na-tional steel companies on bids for public bridge projects. It is the company's specialization that enables it to consistently produce high-quality products, which draws customers back for repeat business. "We are the only producer in Maine that strictly builds bridges. We don't dabble in anything else," says Bryon Tait.

The company starts with raw, American-made steel transported to Maine from North Carolina and trans-forms it into all the steel components needed to con-struct a bridge, from the plate girders and cross frames to expansion joints and steel bridge rail. Casco Bay Steel builds the steel parts in-house and transports them to bridge-building sites across the Northeast.

Many of the bridges that connect small towns and rural parts of New England are built using steel com-ponents fabricated by Casco Bay Steel Structures. With clients ranging from contractors to state departments of transportation, the company plays an integral part in the region's bridges — from new construction proj-ects to bridge upgrades or repair.

The company also is involved in repairing and up-grading urban bridges. Casco Bay Steel most recently completed its first drawbridge in Boston on Route 99 over the Mystic River. "These are very complicated bridges to build, and there are thousands of pieces involved. It took over 20,000 work hours over four months to build the drawbridge," says Bryon Tait. An

upcoming arch bridge project in Worcester, Massachusetts, will be one of the company's biggest projects to date, requiring an estimated 100,000 work hours.

Lately, growing interest in building high-speed rail in the region has helped the company land more railroad projects. For instance, Casco Bay Steel Structures completed a railroad bridge in Stonington, Connecticut, for Amtrak.

Casco Bay Steel Structures has developed strong relationships with the local schools by donating steel to regional vocational programs, such as the Biddeford Regional Center of Technology, and also to the Southern Maine Community College and Portland's Art and Technology High School. A few of the employees at Casco Bay Steel share their passion and experience by teaching courses at Biddeford Regional Center for Technology. The company sees a positive return on investment, often hiring program graduates who have an interest in the industry.

Tait says he is proud to be a Maine employer and credits the company's success to "putting out a good product in a timely manner, which is what a contractor wants." A culture of open communication out on the work floor and up through management reinforces the strong work ethic that Tait used to start the company.

There are a number of employees at Casco Bay Steel who have been with the company for many years, including the company's first employee, who began as a welder and now drives the big rig trucks to deliver the final products to the client. The company values its employees and offers a robust benefits package. Casco Bay Steel pays 100% of every employee's health insurance. Other benefits include 401K, 10 paid holidays per year and vacation accrual time.

Casco Bay Steel Structures Inc. is an AISC certified bridge fabrication company with fracture critical and sophisticated paint endorsements, and is also a member of the National Steel Bridge Alliance.

Top: Little Bay Bridge, Newington-Dover, New Hampshire.

Bottom: Alford Street Bridge, Boston, Massachusetts.

"We are the only producer in Maine that strictly builds bridges. We don't dabble in anything else," says Company Founder Bryon Tait.

Linda Bean's Perfect Maine®

Linda Bean's Maine Lobster Café with lounge has 180-seats for dining and pre-flight relaxation, carry-aboard packed live lobsters, and retail lobster shop for frozen lobster treats, opened in October 2011 at Portland, Maine's International Jetport.

"Linda Bean's Perfect Maine® is a brand name I have chosen to reflect my personal love of my native state," says Linda Bean.

The majority of wild-caught Maine lobsters pass through five hands before being consumed. It begins with fishermen, who sell lobsters directly off-the-boat to a buyer/dealer at the shore. Then the lobsters are transferred to a buyer/grader that sorts, separates and grades them. Next, they are sold and resold into the live market or to a processing plant which cooks and/or freezes them. From there they are shipped into food service for marketing to grocery stores and restaurants.

At their final destination there is one certain outcome: they have gained a far higher price than was paid to the fishermen. It's difficult for many to understand why the hard-working, risk-taking fishermen are paid on average $4 per pound, or sometimes much less, for Maine lobster, when that same lobster, or even just the tail, is eventually served up for $30 to $60.

When Linda Bean decided at age 67 to see what she could do about this, she began by buying her neighbor's business, Bay Lobster Company, in Port Clyde, renaming it Port Clyde Lobster. Linda was trained by David Larson, who had owned and operated Bay Lobster Company for over 20 years and was ready to retire. She set out to do more than simply make a profit by purchasing lobster from fishermen and then selling it to a buyer/grader.

Skipping over the middleman, Bean came up with a way to make an investment that aligned with her instincts: she created a way of sharing the saved dollars with her fishermen, thus creating a lobster trap-to-table business model. The lobster boats and crews are not hers, but her pay policy is designed to keep loyal fishing families in business. Bean's approach has paid off for her fishermen. In 2010, Linda Bean announced that $1.5 million in bonuses were earned by those fishermen.

She also began to think about growing the business to an expanded plateau, including some added value lobster products. She decided to take the business model to a new level and created a creamy lobster bisque for sale on QVC's television network, adding "Bean" to the label to attract customers familiar with her family name and its 95-year history in her home state. After that, Linda developed a secret herb blend to delicately enhance the subtle flavor of sweet lobster meat, advertised her butter-toasted quarter pounder widely, elevated her Maine lobster roll into the national spotlight, and started her own food kiosks and cafés.

Bean decided to put her own brand name on lobster in 2008. By combining the words "Bean," "Maine," and "lobster," she started a very noticeable industry stir. She developed an identification band for each of

PHOTO BY C.A. SMITH PHOTOGRAPHY

her live lobsters, shipped to 2,000 U.S. chain grocery stores. In today's world of savvy shoppers and diners, consumers want to know where their seafood comes from, and Bean decided that any lobsters with her name on them would come only from boats licensed by the state of Maine. She firmly stands her ground to assure buyers that her lobsters are not from Canada or the Caribbean; they are guaranteed 100% Maine caught and processed by proud Maine workers.

In 2009, her 26-foot Lobstermobile was sent on the road to serve Linda's herbed lobster rolls at five Maine state fairs. She created three of her own cafés to serve the herbed lobster roll, one each in Freeport, Camden, and in Portland's Old Port. Additionally, Bean outfitted a 90-seat Linda Bean's Perfect Maine® Lobster Café in Delray Beach, Florida, and licensed a couple to run her lobster roll takeout business on Boston's south shore at Nantasket Beach.

In her third year of business in 2010, Linda purchased and integrated two seafood plants totaling 40,000 square feet in Rockland's industrial park to perform the separation and grading of her lobsters for weight and shippability, and for the cooking and freezing of those too soft-shelled to ship.

By eliminating the middleman and cutting extra costs, she is able to share profits back to fishermen hard-pressed by low prices, producing a model of vertical integration that has captured the attention of at least one U.S. business school. In 2011, Bean and General Manager John Petersdorf paid $1.9 million in bonuses over and above the shore price to fishermen selling to Bean's wharves.

Top: Linda Bean's Americanus Wharf on Vinalhaven Island.

Bottom: Directly across from the L.L.Bean flagship store, Linda Bean's Maine Kitchen & Topside Tavern is a 240-seat, two-story family restaurant in Freeport.

PHOTO BY C.A. SMITH PHOTOGRAPHY

Top: Maine law permits a maximum of 800 traps per licensee. Maine issues about 6,000 licenses, most to boats with two people working aboard.

Bottom: A lobster sports an identification band developed by Linda Bean that verifies the authenticity and location of the Maine dock where the lobster was purchased.

"Our CEO John Petersdorf and I are both thankful for a dedicated working team to make authentic Maine lobster more accessible and affordable to the consumer, which we think is the best formula to help support the Maine lobster industry."

What makes her unique is that she does not send any Maine-caught lobsters to Canada for processing or buy any of theirs when Maine's winter lobsters become scarce. She has her own lobster pound to house live lobsters for winter sales. With other dealers sending more than 70% of Maine-caught lobsters to be processed in Canada, Maine loses in two ways: jobs and brand identity. Bean understands that when Canadian processors buy Maine lobsters cheap and process them in government subsidized plants, she can lose one other way: Canadian companies can afford to undersell her products in volume markets such as American entertainment theme parks and cruise ships. "This is why Maine fishermen get low prices: it's the Canadian problem. Canadian price supports come flooding into our country and seize our markets. It is so unfair to our fishermen," says Bean. "Canada sets the price until we build more plants in Maine, which is stymied by there being no international agreement to level the playing field where each player has an equal chance to succeed."

In 2010, Bean's first frozen seafood product came forth: cooked, in-shell cocktail claws, pre-scored for easy shell removal. An instant hit, it was launched with Walmart in 800 super stores followed by successive annual appearances at Walt Disney World Resort's Epcot theme park where tens of thousands are sold at the International Food & Wine Festival. A great banquet table offering, such as at Maine Governor LePage's inaugural ceremonies, this product required an act of the Maine Legislature to enable the claws

to be pre cut and sold separated from the body. Bean now trademarks the product under the name Maine Lobster Cuddlers®. Packaging wholesale lobster claws, connected to the arms, makes this product available to restaurant chefs nationwide. In retail grocery, the Cuddlers® appear in Bean's colorful nylon-reinforced poly bag.

The company's success was snowballing by 2011, when Linda Bean's Maine Kitchen & Topside Tavern opened in Freeport: a 240-seat restaurant located across the street from her famed grandfather's flagship store, L.L.Bean. The restaurant serves her Maine lobsters, wild-caught Maine shrimp and white fish, Maine meats and vegetables, and homemade pies. A

PHOTO BY C.A. SMITH PHOTOGRAPHY

invited chefs. The culinary creations were a hit, and in her first appearance at the festival, 50,000 herbed lobster rolls were sold in 45 days. Her Epcot festival treats have become favorite menu features in the Freeport restaurant. Linda and her chef's appearances in Maine and Florida are testimonies to the succulence of her authentic, traceable, sustainable, and now affordable Maine lobster and its strong attraction to diners worldwide.

In October 2011, HMSHost opened a new 180-seat lounge and restaurant at the Portland Jetport, Linda Bean's Maine Lobster Café, featuring her family recipes and lobster specialties for the pleasure of air travelers arriving in and departing from Maine's biggest airport gateway. With lobster offerings, even for breakfast, the Jetport location packs carry-on live lobsters for busy travelers, as well as convenient, frozen-packaged meals and treats of Maine lobster and crabmeat, plus Linda's award-winning clam chowder.

In just a few short years, Linda Bean has injected a fresh new approach to the Maine lobster business, hoping to ensure that Maine's lobstering industry will thrive for generations to come. Her focus on making authentic Maine lobster more accessible and affordable to the consumer is central to "Lobster for the 21st Century®," her trademark name and effort to support Maine's lobster industry and its dedicated small boat fishing families.

Top: On one of Linda's three lobster stations at Vinalhaven Island.

Bottom: Linda Bean enjoys her friendships with Maine lobstermen and women.

free Lobster Theater with films and a Touchtank for Kids® was installed next door, to entertain and educate young patrons.

The restaurant's Executive Corporate Chef Andrew Omo introduced Linda Bean's Maine Lobster Mac & Cheese in November 2011 at a culinary demonstration at Disney's Epcot theme park and Linda Bean's Lobster Tails of Joy™ at the festival's November Party for the Senses, an evening event with 20 Disney and

Midcoast Regional Redevelopment Authority

Brunswick Landing is one of the most exciting and desirable real estate locations in New England.

Located at the former Naval Air Station Brunswick, Brunswick Landing and the Brunswick Executive Airport offer prime real estate options for development.

The extraordinary vision of the reuse of the recently closed Naval Air Station Brunswick is a mixed-use development project to benefit the Midcoast region and the State of Maine. This dynamic project includes a world-class executive airport, a business-focused college campus, a number of technology-oriented companies, beautiful residential neighborhoods, and substantial areas set aside for outdoor recreation and conservation, making it one of the most exciting and desirable real estate locations in New England.

The Master Developer of the project is the Midcoast Regional Redevelopment Authority (MRRA), which was established by the State of Maine to manage the transition of the base property from military to civilian use; manage the newest airport in New England; and create new high-quality jobs in innovative industries. MRRA has the ability to either lease or sell buildings and land to quality businesses and real estate developers.

Brunswick Landing: Maine's Center for Innovation is the business hub of the former base property. Brunswick Landing is the State's premier business location with centers of excellence in aerospace, composites and advanced materials, renewable energy, and information technology industries. This beautiful property is a 1,700 acre business campus equipped with state-of-

the-art infrastructure and facilities, possessing over 1.6 million square feet of commercial, industrial and professional office space and a world-class aviation complex, with robust information technology and utility infrastructure, and a public nine-hole golf course.

Brunswick Landing is home to several leading edge companies including: Oxford Networks, Kestrel Aircraft Company and Mölnlycke Health Care with its brand new high-tech manufacturing facility. Mölnlycke Health Care chose to locate its new, state-of-the-art facility at Brunswick Landing because of the extensive existing and planned infrastructure and the vision that MRRA has for developing the property. Maine Technology Institute is located at Brunswick Landing and works with entrepreneurs, innovators, established businesses and institutions conducting research and development to help them fund and grow their big ideas.

The Topsham Commerce Park is located at the former Topsham Annex and offers opportunities for economic and recreation development. With 74 acres of prime real estate nestled within the village of Topsham, Topsham Commerce Park utilizes the existing facilities and infrastructure, providing the framework for a potential redevelopment of the site into a more intensive addition to Topsham's urban landscape. This property offers facilities for professional offices, commercial space and community uses.

The Brunswick Executive Airport (BXM) is a world-class aviation complex that began operating in April 2011. The aviation complex consists of over 650,000 square feet of modern aviation hangar, maintenance and administration space, two 8,000-foot runways and over 100 acres of concrete apron. Other key features of the 1,000-acre airport facility include: Instrument Approaches (ILS and GPS) meeting FAA standards; an advanced glycol recovery de-icing system that exceeds EPA and FAA standards; jet engine test and maintenance facilities; ground support equipment maintenance facilities; and Fixed Base Operator services including fuel, car rental, courtesy car, and tie downs.

Business opportunities at this world-class airport facility include: general and corporate aviation; aircraft manufacturing and maintenance, repair and overhaul; government agencies; and aerospace research and development.

Brunswick Landing hosts the newest campus of Southern Maine Community College (SMCC), providing easy access for continuing education as well as degree and customized training for employers, employees and area residents. Partnering with the University of Maine's College of Engineering, the SMCC campus includes the Maine Advanced Technology and Engineering Center (MATEC) at Brunswick Landing. MATEC collaborates with businesses and industries to establish a well-educated workforce for the businesses at Brunswick Landing as well as throughout the Midcoast region and State of Maine.

In addition, the Town of Brunswick possesses two other colleges, including Bowdoin College and Southern New Hampshire University, offering a broad range of degrees in liberal arts and business. Both are located adjacent to Brunswick Landing.

In order to address the need for affordable renewable and other alternative energy sources, MRRA is developing the Brunswick Renewable Energy Center (BREC). The Center is to be the home of a world-renowned energy complex for integrated research and development, manufacturing, testing, business incubation and the productive operation of green energy technology products and services.

The Brunswick Renewable Energy Center has been established to foster and grow the energy technology cluster in Maine with the opportunity to produce power on site and utilize local and state labor and skills. The BREC is a renewable energy research, development and demonstration living laboratory that combines energy technology business operations with on-site production, distribution and management of energy used within Brunswick Landing itself; a dynamic power demonstration and production facility that allows technologies to evolve; and a center for fostering cutting-edge research.

Several state and federal incentives can assist businesses interested in locating to Brunswick Landing or Topsham Commerce Park, including a reduction in taxes and a variety of exemptions, reimbursements, and credits. In addition, customized workforce training programs can meet the business demands for a highly skilled, technical workforce.

Located within 50 miles of two-thirds of Maine's workforce, Brunswick Landing is an excellent location for business development for a variety of reasons. According to one tenant, "We chose Brunswick Landing because of the infrastructure already in place, along with a well-qualified workforce, including those familiar with composite technology, and a supportive community."

Ribbon cutting at Brunswick Executive Airport April 2011: from left, MRRA Executive Director Steve Levesque, Captain William Fitzgerald, Congressman Mike Michaud, Senator Olympia Snowe, MRRA Board Chair Art Mayo, Senator Susan Collins, Congresswoman Chellie Pingree, and Senator Stan Gerzofsky.

Founded in 2007, the Midcoast Regional Redevelopment Authority (MRRA) is the Master Developer for Brunswick Landing: Maine's Center for Innovation and Topsham Commerce Park.

Asticou Azalea Garden, Northeast Harbor.
David Clough | Rockland

Companies listed by alphabetical order

Contributing Photographers

José Azel
Lovell

Craig M. Becker
Windham

Trent Bell
Portland

Michael Eric Berube
Denmark

Bridget Besaw
Portland

Thomas Birtwistle
Harmony

Peter Bissel
Portland

Alexandria Brahler
Portland

Brendan Bullock
Montville

Jo Chaney
Scarborough

David Clough
Rockland

Matt Cosby
Rockport

Celeste Cota
Brewer

Stacey Cramp
Portland

Paul Cyr
Presque Isle

Don Dunbar
Perry

William Lloyd Duncan
Stockholm

Gifford Ewing
Sorrento

Cynthia Farr-Weinfeld
Portland

Arthur Fink
Portland

Brian Fitzgerald
Portland

Whitney Fox
Peaks Island

Françoise Gervais
Blue Hill

Tim Greenway
Portland

Susan Guthrie
Belfast

Bill Hall
Portland

Sean Harris
Portland

Tanja Hollander
Auburn

Diane Hudson
Portland

Lauren Kennedy
Portland

Alexander Kreher
Portland

Kris Larson
East Machias

Chris Lawrence
Scarborough

Stephen Leighton
Fort Fairfield

Laura "Winky" Lewis
Portland

Carol Liscovitz
Brunswick

Christine Macchi
Dresden

Ben Magro
Appleton

Mark Marchesi
South Portland

David McLain
North Yarmouth

Theodora Medouris
Portland

Roger L. Merchant
Glenburn

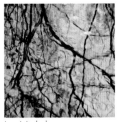

Jim Nickelson
Camden

John Orcutt
Kingfield

Heath Paley
Arundel

Dee Peppe
Rockland

Scott Peterman
Hollis

Peter Ralston
Rockport

Liv Kristin Robinson
Belfast

Ni Rong
Rockport

Jean Pierre Rousset
Gorham

Greta Rybus
Portland

Karl Schatz
Portland

Jeffrey Stevensen
Cape Elizabeth

Corey Templeton
Portland

Jan Pieter van Voorst van
Beest, Pownal

Brian Vanden Brink
Rockport

Carl D. Walsh
Portland

An aged boat with barnacles.
Susan Guthrie | voxphotographs.com | Belfast